MUSIC WORKS

A Handbook of Job Skills for Music Therapists

Revised Edition

Dellinda Henry, RMT-BC

Cathy Knoll, RMT-BC

Barbara Reuer, RMT-BC

Distributed by MUSIC WORKS
1250 Ollie Street, Stephenville, Texas 76401

ISBN: 0-9617272-0-9

ISBN: 0-9617272-1-7

Printed in the United States of America.

TABLE OF CONTENTS

ACKNOWLEDGEMENTS

We wish to express our appreciation to:

Kathleen Coleman and Pam Michel for their input about marketing music therapy services.

Dr. J.W. Donaldson, Executive Director, and Carol T. Gruben, Assistant Director of Special Education, for allowing us to describe and use consultative music therapy forms of Region 18 Education Service Center, Midland, Texas.

Dr. Roger L. Kroth and Richard L. Simpson for permitting the inclusion of workshop interaction activities that they developed to encourage parent-teacher communication.

Kate Gfeller, Marc Cooper, Kathleen Coleman, Barbara Baxley, Suzanne Oliver, and Mark Cowick for permitting us to use samples of their business cards or music therapy brochures.

TAKE A CLOSE LOOK 1

The nature of music therapy lends itself to working with clients of all ages and disabilities. It is this very characteristic that provides music therapists with exciting opportunities as well as challenges. Because of the variety of job possibilities, it is essential that music therapists determine their own unique philosophies, values, and areas of expertise. The following space poses questions to the reader. These questions are not all inclusive, but they should stimulate ideas and help crystallize thoughts.

Are you in the right field?

I chose music therapy as my career because: It provides opportunity for me to teach, use music skills + to help individual overcome or minimize problems

I chose music therapy over other therapies and services because: Music is my skill of choice

If I could choose a career other than music therapy, I would choose: Public School music

Why? I am a musician, a teacher and a "helping" person

What is your personal philosophy about people with handicaps?

I believe people with disabilities can: Live full productive lives, have the right to expect an education and job opportunities as provided for non handicapped person, be accepted by others as peers + equals.

My motivation for working with individuals having handicaps is: They have greatest needs.

What are your personal and professional values?

Check the words that best describe who you are. Circle the areas you would like to improve.

___ Accepting
___ Active
___ Adventurous
___ Ambitious
___ Angry
___ Anxious
___ Appreciative
___ Approachable
___ Articulate
___ Assertive
___ Calm
___ Capable
___ Caring
___ Cautious
___ Committed
___ Communicative
___ Compassionate
___ Competent
___ Competitive
___ Compromising
___ Confident
___ Consistent
___ Contributing
___ Controlling
___ Cooperative
___ Courageous
___ Creative
___ Credible
___ Critical
___ Decisive
___ Dedicated
___ Dependable
___ Determined
___ Dignified
___ Disciplined
___ Discreet
___ Discriminating
___ Efficient

___ Emotional
___ Empathetic
___ Energetic
___ Enterprising
___ Enthusiastic
___ Fair
___ Faithful
___ Far-sighted
___ Fearful
___ Flexible
___ Forgiving
___ Friendly
___ Generous
___ Gentle
___ Genuine
___ Good-natured
___ Guilty
___ Happy
___ Hard-working
___ Healthy
___ Helpful
___ Honest
___ Humble
___ Humorous
___ Imaginative
___ Independent
___ Innovative
___ Insecure
___ Intelligent
___ Lazy
___ Likable
___ Logical
___ Lonely
___ Loving
___ Mature
___ Moody
___ Objective
___ Open-minded

___ Optimistic
___ Organized
___ Patient
___ Perceptive
___ Persistent
___ Persuasive
___ Philosophical
___ Positive
___ Powerful
___ Pragmatic
___ Principled
___ Productive
___ Progressive
___ Purposeful
___ Realistic
___ Reasonable
___ Reflective
___ Relaxed
___ Resourceful
___ Respectful
___ Responsible
___ Secure
___ Self-respecting
___ Sensitive
___ Sincere
___ Sociable
___ Spontaneous
___ Stressed
___ Strong
___ Successful
___ Supportive
___ Thoughtful
___ Tolerant
___ Trusting
___ Unstructured
___ Well-adjusted
___ Worried
___ Youthful

What are your personal priorities and goals?

Area	Number of Priority	Goals
Clubs and Organizations	9	Be reliable
Education	1	complete certification
Family	2	have ongoing close relationship
Finances	1	be solvent (reasonably)
Friends	3	develop network
Geographic Location	5	Would like to settle in T'town
Hobbies and Recreation	10	Attend numerous concerts, etc, socialize
Home	2	Have adequate shelter for time being
Mental Well-being	4	Be confident, stable
Personal Projects	7	Within year complete ongoing photo project
Physical Well-being	4	control diabetes + weight
Sexuality	8	Redefine + hold
Spirituality, Church	6	Maintain strong faith + commitment
Volunteer Projects	11	Not in present plan except in helping individuals in need.

What are your professional priorities and goals?

The handicapping conditions in which I prefer to specialize are: mental + emotional disorders

The types of facilities in which I prefer to work are: psychiatic hospital

I prefer the following type(s) of service delivery:

- [ ] Administration
- [ ] Consultative services
- [x] Direct Services
- [ ] Education
- [x] On-staff employment
- [ ] Research
- [ ] Self-employment
- [ ] Supervision

My personal criteria for job success includes:

- [x] Benefits
- [ ] Choices in geographic location
- [x] Financial security
- [ ] Flexibility in work schedule
- [ ] Job security
- [x] Opportunities for advancement
- [x] Personal fulfillment
- [ ] Other

I will feel successful when: Realize improvement in patient "success", can handle patient involvement, related paper work and maintain an ongoing program.

My short-term professional goals are: Finish certification and return to Bryce Hospital in capacity of RMT

My long-term professional goals are:
Develop a successful MT program and publish in MT journal -

My ultimate goal in life is:
make the world a better place because I have live
(as stated in oratical contest at age 14)

What are your professional strengths and weaknesses?

My education and training include:
B.S. in Education + Certification work - Certification as director of Recreation in NJ

Job and volunteer experience relating to music therapy include: Teacher of music over 27 years; Choir participation + direction over same time period; Director of Recreation at Senior citizen Day Care Program.

I want more training and experience in these areas:
Current certification program areas

I work best in a spirit of ☑ teamwork ☐ competition

☐ a mixture of both.

My professional pet peeves include: not enough time, supplies, staff to do the job -

My current support network consists of:
Professor, supervisor, staff

I am able to use music as a therapeutic tool. YES NO

I am able to adapt therapeutic strategies to meet individual client needs YES NO

I am able to communicate effectively in writing. YES NO

I am able to communicate effectively with staff. YES NO

I am able to communicate effectively with clients. YES NO

I am able to communicate effectively with client families. YES NO

I am able to communicate effectively with professionals outside my work situation. YES NO

In the following areas, I rate myself:

	Good	Adequate	Needs Improvement
Business skills		✓	
Creative thinking	✓		
Decision making	✓		
Dependability	✓		
Energy/Stamina	✓		
Enthusiasm	✓		
Leadership	✓		
Optimism	✓		
Organizational skills	✓		
Perseverance	✓		
Problem solving	✓		

	Good	Adequate	Needs Improvement
Professional image	✓		
Responsibility	✓		
Self-confidence	✓		
Self-discipline		✓	
Self-motivation	✓		
Stress management skills			✓
Time management skills			✓

FINAL NOTE

These questions have been posed to help you identify and prioritize your own beliefs and values. This is an ongoing process. As you develop your own personal and professional values, you will apply these values in various work situations. At the same time, however, recognize that you will encounter professionals with different and sometimes conflicting value systems. In these situations, you must determine if the conflict is detrimental to your own personal or professional values, and then act accordingly.

SUGGESTIONS FOR FURTHER READING

Alexander, J. (1984). Dare to change. New York, NY: New American Library.

Buscaglia, L. F. (1983). The disabled and their parents: A counseling challenge. New York, NY: Holt, Rinehart, and Winston, Limited.

Dyer, W. (Speaker). (1985). Secrets of the universe (Cassette Tape Series). Chicago, IL: Nightingale-Conant Corporation.

Hyatt, C. (1979). The woman's selling game. New York, NY: M. Evans & Co., Inc.

Kohe, J. M. (1979). Your greatest power. Chicago, IL: Success Limited, Inc.

Mandino, O. (1984). The choice. New York, NY: Bantam Books.

Rohn, J. (1981). The seasons of life. Irvine, CA: Discovery Publications.

Ross, S. (1983). Say yes to your potential. Waco, TX: Word Books.

Schiffman, M. (1967). Self-therapy, techniques for personal growth. Berkeley, CA: Wingbow Press.

Schwartz, D. J. (1983). The magic of getting what you want. New York, NY: William Morrow and Co., Inc.

Schwartz, D. J. (1979). The magic of self-direction. New York, NY: Cornerstone Library.

Waitley, D. (1983). Seeds of greatness. Old Tappan, NJ: Fleming H. Revell Co.

The potential for employment of music therapists has yet to be fully explored. In the "traditional" areas such as full-time, on-staff employment by public or private rehabilitation agencies, there are still numerous job options. Other non-traditional job opportunities such as self-employment, contractual arrangements, and consultant services are also increasing in popularity. Facilities that have not utilized music therapy services in the past may open up in the future. Music therapists work as clinicians, clinical supervisors, administrators, educators, and researchers. Exploring all possible client groups, agencies, and types of service delivery allows for making informed choices.

TYPES OF SERVICE DELIVERY

Music therapists are often hired to provide direct services to clients or consultative services to staff, family members, or other professionals. Clinicians may also supervise interns or practicum students. Other jobs involve directing programs or managing direct care staff. In higher educational settings, therapists work as educators, researchers, and clinical supervisors.

Music therapists traditionally work as full-time, permanent staff of an agency. Other options to explore include:

- Contracting services by the hour or day to one or more agencies.
- Hiring one or more music therapists and contracting their services to area agencies. (The managing music therapist may or may not directly supervise the contracted therapists.)
- Presenting in-service workshops and professional growth seminars.
- Working on-staff part-time.
- Working on-staff with flexible hours.
- Working with individuals or small groups of clients in an office, studio, or in the client's home. Payment is made by client, guardians, insurance, or other third party arrangements.

POTENTIAL CLIENTS AND AGENCIES

Public and private residential treatment centers, nursing homes, foster care facilities, public and private schools, and mental health clinics are some of the more traditional agencies employing music therapists. Job opportunities are expanding in general hospitals, wellness centers, prisons, and specialty clinics.

Clients of these agencies may have a variety of different problems, for example:

- Abuse and neglect
- Chronic pain
- Conditions due to aging
- Developmental delay
- Dysfunctional family
- Emotional disturbance
- Failure to thrive, premature birth
- Hearing impairment
- Learning disability
- Mental illness
- Multiple handicaps
- Orthopedic disability
- Physical disability
- Stroke, medical impairment
- Substance abuse
- Terminal illness
- Vision impairment

Before making a final decision as to the type of job to pursue, the music therapist should learn as much as possible about job options in which one is interested. This can be accomplished by observing and talking with working music therapists, by concentrating on specific areas during practicums and clinical internship, and by attending professional growth seminars in related areas.

MAKING A CHOICE

Exploring the pros and cons of viable options helps one see how each job balances with personal and professional priorities and values. One technique for determining pros and cons of job possibilities is to list all points and to compare and contrast the various options. For example, the chart below shows advantages, disadvantages, and specific features of being employed by an agency as compared to being self-employed. The same technique could be used to analyze other job options.

On-Staff Employee	**Self-Employed**
• The on-staff employee is hired by one agency.	• The self-employed music therapist contracts services to one or more agencies.
• The music therapist is hired by an agency on a part-time or full-time basis to provide direct and/or consultative services to its clients and staff.	• The music therapist is self-employed and contracts personally with agencies for direct and/or consultative services.
or	and/or
The music therapist is hired by a central parent agency that contracts the therapist's services to various agencies in the community.	The music therapist provides services to private clients and is reimbursed by the clients.
• Health insurance plans, life insurance plans, social security payments, retirement plans, and credit union opportunities are usually provided.	• The music therapist does his own bookkeeping and taxes and pays his own social security tax, health and hospitalization insurance (if not available through a spouse's employer), and liability insurance.
• The music therapist has paid sick leave and vacation time.	• There may not be provision for paid sick leave or vacation time.
• The music therapist usually has daily access to agency staff and clients.	• The music therapist may have reduced access to agency staff and clients due to the contract status.

On-Staff Employee	Self-Employed
• The therapist may be called upon to see vast numbers of clients served by the agency.	• The therapist has control over the work schedule, number of clients, types of agencies.
• The agency must make a financial commitment of salary and benefits over a long period of time when creating staff positions for a music therapist.	• An agency can contract for the number of hours it can afford when it is unable to fund a full-time staff position.
• The therapist has a yearly budget with which to purchase equipment and supplies and an office or central work area to use daily.	• The therapist will need to maintain a central home or studio office. Contracting agencies may or may not provide equipment, supplies, and other support.
• The on-staff employee may disagree with certain agency policies and procedures.	• The self-employed music therapist must have self-discipline to work effectively in a situation that is largely unstructured and unsupervised.

FINAL NOTE

There are numerous options for employment in music therapy. While some jobs are easily attained, others are created only through perseverance. Working as a music therapist can be both personally satisfying and financially rewarding, especially when the job complements one's current interests, life situation, and individual needs.

SUGGESTIONS FOR FURTHER READING

Steele, A.L. (1975). A look at contractual arrangements. Journal of Music Therapy. 12(3), 147-154.

Steele, A.L. (1977). Directive teaching and the music therapist as consultant. Journal of Music Therapy. 14(1), 17-26.

When seeking new employment or a change in jobs, a marketing plan is essential. Marketing music therapy services involves developing a quality program, targeting potential consumers, and communicating effectively with those consumers. Thorough preparation can make the difference between success and failure.

OFFER A QUALITY PRODUCT

The first step in advance preparation is to develop skills as a therapist and musician through a quality education and experience in the field. Take advantage of professional growth opportunities:

- Attend conferences, workshops, and classes related to the field.
- Join related professional and support organizations.
- Observe other music therapists and professionals at work.
- Review relevant books and periodicals regularly.

DEFINE CAREER GOALS AND OBJECTIVES

The next step in advance planning is to specify short-term and long-term career goals. The therapist must consider personal priorities and values when defining job-related goals. Once the music therapist knows the general direction of one's career path, a move toward employment can be made with confidence and purpose.

LOCATE AND ASSESS POTENTIAL EMPLOYERS

Sources for locating social service agencies in a community include:

- Civil Service offices
- Directors of United Way agencies
- Local Chamber of Commerce
- Local and regional chapters of support groups
- National and regional newsletters of social service organizations
- State employment services
- Yellow pages of the telephone directory

Talking with music therapists and other allied health professionals in the area is often helpful.

Touring prospective facilities gives the music therapist an opportunity to obtain general information about the agency structure, clientele, and programs currently being offered. Immediately after visiting an agency, write down ideas as to ways music therapy can enhance the existing program. Such information is helpful when approaching administrators later.

Some agencies are structured in such a way that funding is provided for services such as music therapy **only** if requests for those services are made by a client, family member, case worker, teacher, or other direct care provider and included on the client's treatment plan. The music therapist should discuss the benefits and availability of music therapy with direct care personnel to assure that the necessary request for services is made prior to quarterly or yearly program planning conferences.

Knowing the name of the administrator who makes programming decisions as well as the individual who requests the provision of specific services is valuable when approaching an agency about a new music therapy program. The following are sample titles to watch for:

- Activities or recreation specialist
- Contract services director
- Executive or assistant director
- Music department supervisor
- Parent liaison
- Program coordinator or supervisor
- Rehabilitation services coordinator

- Related services coordinator
- Special education director
- Special services coordinator
- Superintendent or assistant superintendent of pupil services
- Support services coordinator

In developing a new job position, the music therapist is advised to investigate the agency's fiscal calendar and deadlines for budget planning. This information will prevent the applicant from approaching the potential employer after the agency's finances are firmly committed. Likewise, the employed music therapist should be aware of these dates when requesting funds for equipment, program expansion, or additional staff. Sometimes there may be excess funds available at the end of an agency's fiscal year.

MAKE YOURSELF VISIBLE

A successful marketing strategy utilizes many channels when introducing music therapy services to the market. Attend meetings of professional, educational, and allied health groups, advocate and parent support organizations, and other community service groups. Presenting prepared public awareness programs to various groups can be a good introduction to people concerned with disabled individuals in a community. An article about music therapy or a notice of the availability of services might be included in newsletters of organizations and allied health service agencies. Some newspapers and local television stations will accept articles and stories with broad public appeal that can increase public awareness of music therapy. Music therapy services could be included on lists of local services published by the Chamber of Commerce or public service agencies.

Posting flyers, brochures, or business cards in key areas increases public awareness of a new program. Community bulletin boards in churches, community recreation centers, senior citizen centers, libraries, daycare centers, schools, stores, manufacturing plants, and other high traffic areas are good possibilities for free advertising. Always ask permission to post information to avoid any misunderstandings.

Several options for advertising that require a greater financial commitment include bulk mailings of brochures or formal announcements, and paid advertisements in newspapers, neighborhood shopper's guides, area magazines, and other publications. Advertisements should specify services offered, clientele, credentials, and contact information. Before any money is spent on advertising, the music therapist should analyze the market by locating potential clients and determining the most effective ways of reaching them.

DEVELOP MARKETING MATERIALS

Materials that introduce the music therapist and explain available services might include a resume, information brochure, program proposal, videotapes, business cards, advertisements, and formal announcements. Such materials are used to communicate objective facts and ideas and to capture the attention of the reader. Therefore, be cognizant of the quality of information, typing, printing, and paper. Well-written materials will make an immediate impression upon a prospective employer.

When developing written materials, outline the important points, then write the information concisely and clearly in an easy-to-read format. Leave adequate margins, list facts, and emphasize key points with headings.

Letterheads make written communication look professional. Letterhead paper can be designed by oneself or by a commercial artist using musical symbols, special lettering, or a music therapy related picture. A more economical way of personalizing a form is with a rubber stamp. The style of letterhead or artwork used reflects upon the music therapist and the quality of work performed.

Resume

The purpose of a resume is to win an interview, not a job (that happens at the interview). Items included on a resume are name, address, phone, experience, and education. Information such as personal data, salary requirements, reasons for leaving previous jobs, photographs, and health information are not appropriate.

Use factual, clear and concise language. Action verbs such as edited, reorganized, and trained are effective. A professional resume is one or two pages long, and is neat without "cute" letterheads or gimmicks. Have a friend critique the final product, making sure the information shows motivation, confidence, initiative, dependability, and good judgment through work experience descriptions.

A brief cover letter addressed to a person rather than a title should accompany a resume. The letter might include a job objective. Although the letter need not repeat any information in the resume, it might show how some background or experiences relate to the agency's program or clients.

Business Letters

Before writing a business letter, one should write down the main purpose of the letter and the details of all points to be covered. Prioritize each item, omitting any offensive or weak details. When writing the body of the letter, approach the topics from the viewpoint of the reader of the letter. After the rough draft is completed, check these points:

- Will the first sentence make the reader want to continue?
- Are all the facts stated immediately? Clearly?
- Is bad news conveyed after reassurance of cooperation and good will?
- Are the facts stated step by step?
- Do the facts sound biased?
- Is one idea used for one sentence? One idea per paragraph?
- Does the letter state specifically and clearly what the writer wants?
- Is correct grammar, punctuation, and spelling used?
- Are there unnecessary words, outdated phrases?
- Are there action verbs?
- Is the letter easy to read?
- Can the letter be misunderstood?
- Is the letter visually attractive?
- Is the expression correct, concise, natural, and fluid?
- Is the tone friendly and professional?
- Does the letter reflect a sincere attitude?
- Are all terms defined and abbreviations explained?

DIRECT CONTACT WITH AN AGENCY

Initial contact with a prospective agency may be in the form of a letter followed by a phone call. The initial approach letter should be accompanied by a resume, a brochure or packet of information about music therapy in general, and a list of local agencies utilizing music therapy services if appropriate. The body of the letter should introduce the therapist, explain the purpose for the contact, outline some options for inservice or pilot programs for the agency, and request an interview. Imply a spirit of cooperation rather than competition. Do not appear dependent upon the agency for a successful music therapy business or job. Try to imply the attitude: "It would be nice if you contracted with or hired me, but I have other options." Offer to assist in providing services. Keep the administration informed of your professional involvement with their clients/students.

If the administrator expresses some interest in the program, an appointment for an interview might be scheduled. The purpose of the interview is to learn more about the place of employment and to give information about yourself to the potential employer. Review the "Job Interview Checklist" at the end of this chapter.

When interviewing in an agency without a music therapy position, be prepared to give a brief explanation of music therapy and to discuss the ways music therapy would enhance the agency's program, meet specific client needs, and provide cost-effective programming. A written outline of these points as well as options in program structure and funding possibilities is a useful communication tool.

Creative thinking is important in exploring funding options. The therapist could be hired full-time, part-time, on-staff, or on a contractual basis. Monies for a program may come from:

- Agency's general budget
- Client payments
- Contractual personnel budgets
- Grant or foundation funds
- Music education budget
- Non-profit organization donations
- Private monies or donations
- Third-party reimbursements

Up-to-date information about public and private funds, and hints for writing proposals is available from catalogues, journals, and newsletters. A list of resources is on page 28.

"WHEN ALL ELSE FAILS"

After an unsuccessful attempt to gain employment, review goals and options, make changes if necessary, and formulate a new plan of action. Several alternatives are possible in such a situation.

Follow-Up: Maintain communication with the agency's staff and try again when the time is right. When approaching an agency for the second time, propose a different alternative for funding and/or implementation of music therapy for their consideration.

Pilot Programs: Short term music therapy pilot programs provided at no charge to the agency demonstrate the value of music therapy to the staff and administrators. The music therapist can gain valuable experience and contacts with staff and clients; the administrators can learn more about the program before making a permanent financial commitment.

Move-On: Contact other agencies in the community. A "second choice" agency may become an unexpected and favorable work opportunity.

When job possibilities seem bleak, the music therapist should remember:

- Avoid panic. It distorts logical thinking and inhibits creation of new alternatives.
- Determine if the goal and sacrifices necessary to obtain that goal will be worth the current discomforts.
- Find an emotional support system.
- Have faith.
- Remember that retail businesses initially operate in the red; the marketing of a professional service also takes time to develop and become profitable.
- Talk with other music therapists who have experienced similar situations.

FINAL NOTE

If your employment situation is unsuccessful, do not consider yourself a failure. The only failure is in not taking advantage of employment opportunities open to you. There is growth in being able to say, "It's not for me," and exploring new options for employment.

SUGGESTIONS FOR FURTHER READING

Bates, J.D. (1985). Writing with precision. Washington, D.C.: Acropolis.

Camden, T. (Speaker). (1985). Get that job (How to cure unemployment). (Cassette Tape Series). Chicago, IL: Nightingale-Conant Corporation.

Cooper, P.D., Kehoe, W.J., & Murphy, P.E. (1978). Marketing and preventive health care: Interdisciplinary and interorganizational perspectives. Chicago, IL: American Marketing Association.

Dickut, H. (1981). The professional resume and job search guide. Englewood Cliffs, NJ: Prentice-Hall, Inc.

Edwards, F.G. (1983). Marketing of professional services. Palo Alto, CA: Louis A. Allen Associates, Inc.

Frederiksen, L.W., Solomon, L.J., & Brehony, K.A. (1984). Marketing health behavior: Principles, techniques, and applications. New York, NY: Plenum Press.

Hamilton, P.A. (1982). Health care consumerism. St. Louis, MO: The C.V. Mosby Company.

Hamner, J.E. & Sax Jacobs, B.J. (1983). Marketing and managing health care: Health promotion and disease prevention. Memphis, TN: The University of Tennessee, Center for the Health Services.

Kotler, P. (1982). Marketing for non-profit organizations (2nd ed.). Englewood Cliffs, NJ: Prentice-Hall, Inc.

Mac Stravic, R.E. (1980). Marketing by objectives for hospitals. Germantown, MD: Aspen Systems Corporation.

Mager, N.H. & Mager, S.K. (1980). What to say & how to say it. New York, NY: William Morrow & Co., Inc.

Melillo, J.V. (Ed.). (1983). Market the arts! New York, NY: Foundation for the Extension and Development of the American Professional Theater.

Rothman, J., Teresa, J.G., Key, T.L., & Morningstar, G.C. (1983). Marketing human service innovations (Vol. 146). Beverly Hills, CA: Sage Publications, Inc.

White, V. (Ed.). (1983). Grants proposals that succeeded. New York, NY: Plenum Press.

Williams, T.A. & Johnson, J.A. (Eds.). (1979). Mental health in the twenty-first century. Lexington, MA: D. C. Heath & Company.

Winston, W.J. (Ed.). (1983). Practical methods for the health care practitioner. In Marketing the group practice. New York, NY: Haworth Press.

Winston, W.J. (Ed.). (1984). Marketing for mental health services. New York, NY: Haworth Press.

RESOURCES FOR FUNDING INFORMATION*

Catalog of Federal Domestic Assistance, Superintendent of Documents, Government Printing Office, Washington, D.C. 20402

Directory of National Information Sources on Handicapping Conditions and Related Services, Clearinghouse on the Handicapped, Office of Special Education and Rehabilitative Services, Department of Education, Switzer Building, Room 3132, Washington, D.C. 20202

The Foundation Center, 79 Fifth Avenue, New York, NY 10003

Guidelines: Clinical Investigator and Academic/Teacher Awards (brochure), Office of Grants Inquiries, Division of Research Grants, National Institutes of Health, Bethesda, MD 20205

Information from the NIH on Grants and Contracts (brochure), Office of Grants Inquiries, Division of Research Grants, National Institutes of Health, Bethesda, MD 20205

National Rehabilitation Information Center (NARIC), School of Library and Information Science, Catholic University of America, 4407 Eighth Street, N.E., Washington, D.C. 20017

Office for Special Constituencies, National Endowment for the Arts, 1100 Pennsylvania Avenue, N.W., Washington, D.C. 20506

OSERS News in Print (quarterly newsletter), Clearinghouse on the Handicapped, Office of Special Education and Rehabilitative Services, Department of Education, Switzer Building, Room 3132, Washington, D.C. 20202

SPECIALNET, National Association of State Directors of Special Education, 2021 K Street, N.W., Suite 315, Washington, D.C. 20006

Whole Non Profit Catalog, The Grantsmanship Center, 1031 South Grand Avenue, P. O. Box 15072, Los Angeles, CA 90015-0072

*Source: Rohrbacher, M. (Editor). Promoting Arts Therapies, P. O. Box 389063, Cincinnati, Ohio 45238.

SAMPLE

INFORMATION BROCHURE

Source: Barbara L. Baxley, RMT

SAMPLE FORMAT

INFORMATION BROCHURE

(for an Agency)

DEFINITION OF MUSIC THERAPY: (Based upon the agency's and music therapist's philosophies.)

PRIMARY GOALS OF MUSIC THERAPY PROGRAM:

RESPONSIBILITIES OF THE MUSIC THERAPIST:

CLIENTELE:

REFERRAL PROCESS:

SERVICE DELIVERY STYLES:

SUPERVISORY STRUCTURE:

MUSIC THERAPY OFFICE ADDRESS:

SAMPLE FORMAT

INFORMATION BROCHURE

(for Self-Employed Music Therapist)

DEFINITION OF MUSIC THERAPY: (Based upon the music therapist's training and philosophy.)

WHAT DOES MUSIC THERAPY HAVE TO OFFER A FACILITY?

WHAT ARE THE QUALIFICATIONS OF A REGISTERED MUSIC THERAPIST?

BIOGRAPHICAL INFORMATION ABOUT MUSIC THERAPIST:

FOR INFORMATION, CONTACT:

SAMPLE

Cathy Knoll REGISTERED MUSIC THERAPIST

Box T428 Stephenville, Texas 76402 817/968-2882

MUSIC THERAPY

DEFINITION: Music therapy is the use of music learning experiences specifically designed to assist the handicapped individual by modifying ineffective learning patterns and inappropriate behavioral patterns. Music therapy in an educational setting focuses on the following areas: classroom survival skills, social skills, auditory perceptual skills, self-concept, perceptual motor skills, language skills, and basic academic concepts.

MUSIC THERAPY PROGRAM PLANNING: Music therapy goals and objectives coincide with those of the classroom teacher and other related services, thereby providing an additional opportunity and method for students to make progress in target areas. Specific programs and procedures are planned for the students, and records of student progress are kept. The therapist shares this information with parents, teachers, and others who are involved in the student's well-being and development.

DIRECTIVE TEACHING: Most individuals acquire interests and skills through established curricula and teaching procedures. For many, certain conditions interfere with expected learning patterns. These difficulties may be associated with learning disabilities, developmental disabilities, emotional or behavioral problems, or physical handicaps. Similar difficulties may be noted with the "poorly motivated" child or the "rebellious" adolescent. In directive teaching, the music therapist develops an individualized program for each student that encourages him to learn at his own pace and reinforces any progress he makes. The student not only develops useful skills in this manner; but he can also develop greater confidence and self-esteem.

THE THERAPIST: Cathy Knoll is a Registered Music Therapist who has a degree in music therapy with honors from Texas Woman's University. She completed her music therapy internship at The Cleveland Music School Settlement in Cleveland, Ohio. After becoming registered with the National Association for Music Therapy, Cathy worked on the staff at Cleveland with a variety of agencies on a contractual basis. She worked with emotionally disturbed, retarded, learning disabled, deaf, and physically handicapped children, and with both retarded and emotionally disturbed adults. She also coordinated an early intervention program with "normal" first graders in public schools. In 1975, Cathy moved to Kerrville, Texas, where she established a music therapy program at the Texas Center for the Blind. Since 1978, Cathy has been contracting music therapy services to agencies and private clients in Stephenville, Granbury, and Glen Rose. She has published articles in regional and national professional journals about music therapy and teaching music to the handicapped. She has presented workshops at numerous regional and national professional conferences. Cathy is a co-author of <u>MUSIC WORKS, A Handbook of Job Skills for Music Therapists</u>, Revised Edition.

"a program responsive to special needs"

SAMPLE

MUSIC THERAPY
(A Program Responsive to Special Needs)

Private and group instruction by a Registered Music Therapist is offered at reasonable rates to children, adolescents, and adults with mental or physical handicaps.

Cathy Knoll, RMT
968-2882

Creative music and crafts workshops also available for pre-school children.

Creative Music Classes

A special new program for pre-school and primary grade children that combines music learning with fun. Individualized programs help each child develop skills and reach his maximum potential.

Cathy Knoll, RMT
968-2882

- Guitar and Piano instruction available for all ages.
- Special classes for physically or mentally handicapped children or adults.

PIANO INSTRUCTION OR MUSIC THERAPY
by
DELLINDA HENRY, RMT

Piano and Music Theory
Music Therapy Services
Beginning Guitar

Services offered by a member of the
Austin District Music Teacher's Association
and
Registered by the
National Association for Music Therapy

Philosophy
MUSIC - A TOOL FOR LEARNING NON-MUSIC SKILLS
MUSIC - SOMETIMES A CAREER, ALWAYS A DAILY EXPERIENCE

For information and registration, call
Dellinda Henry
454-0147

SAMPLE

MUSIC THERAPY

Responsive to the Needs of Children
With Mental or Physical Handicaps

Through the medium of music, this program helps develop:

* language skills
* social skills
* academic skills

Registered music therapists will provide:

* small group sessions
* individual sessions

Kathleen Coleman, RMT
Pam Michel, RMT
498-4067

Sessions begin in May and will continue through the summer.

SAMPLE

BUSINESS CARDS

(817) 498-4067 (METRO)

KATHLEEN A. COLEMAN, RMT
REGISTERED MUSIC THERAPIST

INDIVIDUAL OR GROUP THERAPY
FOR CHILDREN WITH
SPECIAL NEEDS

MARC COOPER

ILLUSTRATION
CALLIGRAPHY
DESIGN

451-1190

1900 WEST 40TH
AUSTIN, TEXAS 78731

Kate E. Gfeller, Ph.D.
Assistant Professor

The University of Iowa
Iowa City, Iowa 52242

School of Music
(319) 353-3825

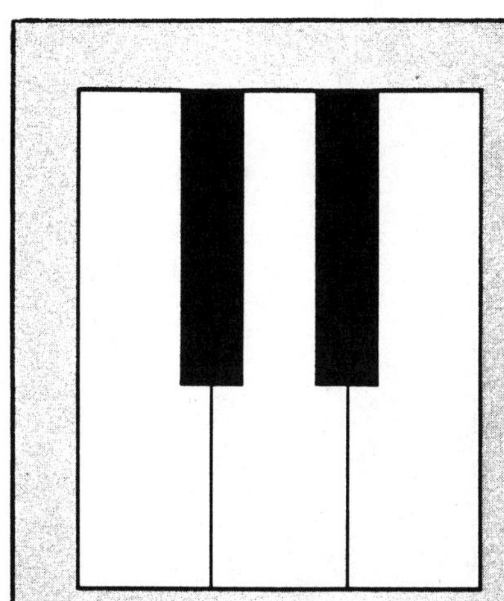

PIANO & HARPSICHORD
TUNING & REPAIR
472-2865
MARK COWICK
CRAFTSMAN MEMBER OF THE
PIANO TECHNICIANS' GUILD

Music Therapy
Services
of Arizona

P.O. Box 25798
Tempe, Arizona 85282
Phone: (602) 241-8409

Suzanne Oliver, R.M.T.-B.C.
Registered Music Therapist
Board Certified

SAMPLE

AMY L. ROBACH, M.A.

WISHES TO ANNOUNCE THAT SHE IS NOW ENGAGED
IN THE PRIVATE PRACTICE OF SPEECH PATHOLOGY
WITH OFFICES AT

WESTWAY MEDICAL BUILDING
1469 PARK EAST
BAYWIND, OHIO

346-4084

VINCENT L. FIERO, RMT-BC

IS PLEASED TO ANNOUNCE THE OPENING OF OFFICES
AT THE CENTER FOR ATTITUDINAL HEALING
1003 Washington Parkway at Main
Jackson, Missouri

MUSIC THERAPY SERVICES

BY APPOINTMENT 226-4342

RESUME

NAME:

ADDRESS:

PHONE:

EMPLOYMENT OBJECTIVE:

PRESENT EMPLOYMENT: (date started)
  Agency:
  Address:
  Position:
  Job Responsibilities:

PREVIOUS EMPLOYMENT: (date started - date ended)
  Agency:
  Address:
  Position:
  Job Responsibilities:

EDUCATION:

REGISTRATION AND CERTIFICATION:

CLINICAL TRAINING:
  INTERNSHIP: (date started - date ended)
    Agency:
    Address:
    Intern Supervisor:

  PRACTICUM EXPERIENCE:
    Agency: (date started - date ended)
    Supervisor:
    Population:
    Time Spent:
    Responsibilities:

  PRACTICUM EXPERIENCE:
    Agency: (date started - date ended)
    Supervisor:
    Population:
    Time Spent:
    Responsibilities:

PROFESSIONAL AFFILIATIONS: (include committees, etc.)

PUBLICATIONS:

CONFERENCE PRESENTATIONS:

REFERENCES:

SAMPLE

Specific call

INITIAL CONTACT LETTER

Date

Name, Title
Agency
Address

Dear Name:

I will graduate in May from the National College of Music Therapy with a degree in music therapy. My particular interest lies in the use of music therapy in the education of the handicapped. If you are unfamiliar with music therapy in public education, it is basically the use of special music strategies to aid a child's progression in designated skill areas. In Texas public education, music therapy is designated as a related service, the same as Occupational Therapy and Physical Therapy.

Currently, I am an intern in the Rosewood and Finsley school districts. The music therapy services provided in these areas have proven to be very effective, and it is my belief that your program could also be further enhanced with the addition of a music therapist.

I am seeking contractual work in public school special education programs for next year. For your consideration, I would like to offer a few options that may help you become more familiar with music therapy as a related service in special education. I can give an inservice in your district for your special education teachers, or make a presentation for a parent support group. Another option that I can provide is a pilot program conducted with specific students in one of your schools for a six week period. I am open to however your district can best be served.

I would like to meet with you and discuss these as well as any other program proposals for your school district in further detail. Please review my resume, and contact me if you have any questions.

Sincere regards,

make arrangements to call

make call

Name
Address
Phone Number

Enclosure (Resume)

SAMPLE

FOLLOW UP LETTER TO A PHONE CALL

Date

Name
Title
Agency
Address

Dear Name:

I enjoyed talking with you during my phone call on December 17th. It was my understanding that although you feel that music therapy is very effective in special education, your district may be too small at this time to have its own music therapy program. I can understand your concern; however, I would like to point out that the Stevenson and Faslow school districts west of the metroplex have a music therapist contracting services to their special education programs. They are small districts as well.

As a small school district, one option might be to contract direct and consultative services in music therapy for just one day per week. This day could include 5 hours of direct service to students (10 thirty minute sessions), and 2 hours of consultative services for teachers. At a $25.00 hourly rate, the total cost to you would be a maximum of $175.00 a week for up to 50 contract hours with students. There is no charge for school holidays or my absences. Other agencies have found these direct service contracts very cost effective. As the district grows, more music therapy services can be added as the budget allows.

A handout of additional information about music therapy in special education is enclosed. I hope you will find it helpful. Feel free to contact any of the references listed. These agencies are currently contracting music therapy services in this area.

Sincerely,

Name
Address
Telephone Number

Enclosures

SAMPLE

after letter response letter

FOLLOW UP LETTER TO A RESPONSE

Date

Name, Title
Agency
Address

Dear Name:

I was happy to receive your letter of December 12th. It would be a pleasure for me to provide any information on music therapy and its use with exceptional children that you believe would be helpful to you. In response to your questions, music therapy is used beneficially with a variety of handicapping conditions either in small groups or individually. Music is motivating, and many special children may respond to it before they ever respond with language, vocalizations, or even eye contact. Particularly important in music therapy are imitation skills. These skills lead to language development, which in turn leads to the development of cognitive skills. Also, the fine and gross motor skills needed to play instruments, a highly motivating activity, aid in the improvement of perceptual skills such as body awareness, directionality, and eye-hand coordination. These are only a few of the goals which are included in the State's prescribed essential elements.

As you requested, I have compiled some information for your review, including information on music therapy and its practice in our area special education programs, several journal articles, and a bibliography of suggested readings. Also, you may find the video tape and its accompanying paper especially interesting. It is my internship supervisor's thesis project for her master's degree in music therapy. I hope that you are able to view this video, since seeing music therapy in action may be the most helpful means for understanding it. In addition, I am presently working with some of the children that you will see on the tape.

I hope this information is helpful to you. I look forward to meeting with you and discussing music therapy further, and more specifically how it might be incorporated into your present program. At that time I would like to pick up the video tape so that I may return it to my supervisor, since she was so gracious to allow me to loan it to you.

Please contact me if you desire information on anything which I have not provided. I hope we will be able to meet soon. Until then, have a happy holiday season. I will call for an appointment after the holidays.

Sincere regards,

Pamela H. Michel
Address
Telephone Number

SAMPLE FORMAT

PROPOSAL FOR MUSIC THERAPY SERVICES

I. WHY USE MUSIC THERAPY? BACKGROUND INFORMATION. ESTABLISH NEED FOR SERVICES.

II. COST-EFFECTIVENESS

III. GOALS AND OBJECTIVES

IV. REFERRAL PROCESS

V. CLIENTELE

VI. SPACE AND EQUIPMENT REQUIREMENTS

VII. SUPPORT STAFF REQUIREMENTS

VIII. FINANCIAL CONCERNS

IX. REPORT SUBMITTED BY: (Name, Address, Telephone Number)

THE JOB INTERVIEW CHECKLIST

Preparation

____ Have several copies of your resume.

____ Prepare pertinent questions you want to ask.

____ Be ready to elaborate on resume: qualifications, experience, and previous job responsibilities.

____ Be prepared to explain any weaknesses and your plan for overcoming them.

____ Know the salary scale for your area; be prepared to state the salary you require.

____ Have ample time for the interview. Do not schedule other things before or after the appointment.

____ Have appropriate marketing materials if proposing a new job position (program proposal, brochure, business card).

The Actual Interview

____ Dress appropriately.

____ Arrive mentally prepared.

____ Have a solid handshake.

____ Listen to the employer and maintain eye contact.

____ Give a clear idea of your preferences regarding the job.

____ Avoid criticizing former employers or co-workers.

____ State reasons for leaving a job via your own goals rather than weaknesses of your former employer.

____ Tactfully refuse to answer inappropriate questions.

____ Be certain of salary, benefits, and duties before leaving.

____ Ask when you may expect a decision or when you may call to inquire about the employer's decision.

____ Make a written note of time, date, and place for a second interview or a request for additional information.

____ Thank the interviewer for his or her time and interest.

____ Do not discuss your personal, domestic, or financial problems unless specifically asked.

____ Do not be afraid to ask the interviewer questions.

____ Do not feel forced to accept a job at the time of interview.

____ Do not show embarrassment in discussing salary.

Self-Evaluation After the Interview

____ Did I talk too much or too little?

____ Was I too aggressive or not assertive enough?

____ What questions caught me completely off-guard?

____ How can I improve my next interview?

Workshops and awareness presentations are useful public relations and job development tools. Presentations at seminars and conferences are opportunities for sharing ideas and experiences with colleagues. Agencies are often willing to pay for professional growth presentations appropriate for their personnel, giving therapists opportunities for supplementary income. A successful presentation requires careful planning in the areas of content, style, and technical details.

CONTENT

It is important to consider the background and interests of the audience and to determine what knowledge and/or specific skills they will gain from the presentation. A "Presentation Information Sheet," similar to the one found on page 50, can clarify goals and content expectations.

Examples of presentation topics that have been successful for music therapists are as follows:

- Behavioral Techniques in Music Therapy
- Creative Funding for Music Therapy Programs

- How Music Therapy Can Benefit the Clients in Your Agency
- Including Music in Your Recreational Activities Program
- Mainstreaming -- How to Make It Work
- Music Activities Workshop (for specialized populations)
- Music and Your Emotions
- Music Therapy in Early Childhood
- Music Therapy: What the Administrator Needs to Know
- Musical Approaches to Child Development
- Overview of Music Therapy
- Support Services: How Do They Relate?
- Using Music to Develop Language
- Using Music to Reinforce Academic Skills

A detailed outline including estimated time spans for each section of the presentation is an effective planning tool. Activity, listening, and group discussion sections should be sequenced to provide variety and maintain interest. Planning one or more flexible sections (sections that can easily be shortened or lengthened in time) is helpful and often necessary.

A creative, non-threatening introductory activity may help stimulate interest. Music activities certainly assist the music therapist in defining the mood of a presentation. Get-acquainted or warm-up activities are also beneficial. Examples of non-musical interaction activities are provided at the end of this chapter.

Brief, understandable definitions of music therapy are generally more effective than lengthy book definitions. A history of music therapy may or may not be interesting depending on the audience. Slide presentations or activities demonstrating actual examples of therapy in action are valuable to persons unfamiliar with music therapy.

The use of professional jargon is appropriate only if participants are familiar with the terminology. Communicating ideas clearly is the presentor's primary concern. To assure clarity, either avoid using jargon, or define terms in advance and/or simultaneously with their use.

PRESENTATION METHODS

Credibility must be earned. The music therapist must demonstrate professionalism by dress, oral presentation, and interaction with participants. When responding to questions, the presentor should not hesitate to say, "I don't know." Avoid responding sarcastically to uninformed comments or questions.

The music therapist may wish to consider team or panel presentations in lengthy workshops. A partner can provide feedback, share the workload, fill in during emergencies, and provide variety for the participants. A partner should be chosen carefully according to their attitudes, professionalism, and expertise. Professionals outside the field of music therapy are frequently helpful. For example, administrators of agencies with music therapy programs can aid the therapist in a presentation based on job development or speech pathologists could be helpful when presenting a workshop on music and language.

The presentation style depends largely upon the needs of the participants. The music therapist will hopefully establish a comfortable climate that allows the participants to relax and feel free to ask questions or share ideas. If the numbers, backgrounds, and/or needs of the people attending the presentation can be controlled, the workshop can be a more effective learning experience for all. During the presentation, the therapist will need to begin punctually, stay on the topic, and end on time. Possible amenities to consider may include name tags, refreshments, and/or background music before and after the program.

The music therapist should give careful thought to handouts, audio-visual aids, and displays. Effective use of a variety of materials allows the participants to learn through many channels. Handouts vary in format and content; some are outlines while others are narratives. Usually, music therapists develop their own slide presentations or video tapes.

Presentation evaluation forms completed by those attending are used to aid the music therapist in planning future presentations and determining the value of topics. Concise checklists with space for comments make completing the form easy for the participants and compiling evaluation information easy for the presenter. Feedback evaluations should ask questions appropriate and pertinent to the type of presentation being given. Workshop planning guides and suggested formats for handouts and evaluation forms are located at the end of this chapter.

PRACTICAL CONSIDERATIONS

Anticipating all emergencies such as faulty equipment and attending to details such as an adequate supply of handouts can contribute to the success of a presentation. Arrangements for the provision of audio-visual aids and equipment should be made well in advance. All audio-visual aids should be previewed and equipment checked prior to the presentation, preferably with a technician nearby to offer simple mechanical suggestions for improving operational quality. Spare projector bulbs and extension cords should also be available. Being familiar with basic equipment usage and maintenance procedures is extremely important if you deliver many presentations. The media departments of various agencies and colleges offer workshops of this nature.

Physical facilities are an important consideration as well. The room should be large enough to accommodate the anticipated number of participants and equipped with a sufficient supply of tables and comfortable chairs. A pleasant room temperature and adequate lighting will allow participants to concentrate on the program rather than their physical comfort.

Allow as much pre-program preparation time as possible. Arriving early gives the presenter an opportunity to check room arrangements, equipment, and other details without the pressure of time. Even if nothing can be done to remedy a problem, the music therapist may be able to revise the presentation to improve the situation.

FINAL NOTE

Many professionals hesitate to make presentations because they lack confidence and public speaking experience. One way to build confidence is to organize a panel to present a program for a local organization. This style of presenting is less threatening than a solo professional conference presentation, and the experience is invaluable. Some therapists find planning and presenting workshops rewarding in that they organize thoughts and ideas, set the occasion for feedback from the audience, and facilitate the therapist's own professional growth.

SUGGESTIONS FOR FURTHER READING

Davis, L. (1974). Planning, conducting, and evaluating workshops. Austin, TX: Learning Concepts.

Linver, S. (1978). Speak easy. New York, NY: Summit Books.

Lorghary, J. & Hopson, B. (1979). Producing workshops, seminars, and short courses. Chicago, IL: Associated Press, Follett Publishing Company.

Micali, P. (1975). How to put yourself across. New York, NY: Hawthorn Books, Inc.

Schmidt, R. (1965). How to speak with confidence. New York, NY: Frederick Fell, Inc.

SAMPLE

PRESENTATION INFORMATION SHEET

1. Date of Contact:
   Date of Presentation:
   Time of Presentation:
   Sponsoring Organization:
   Fee/Contract:
2. Initial Contact Person:
   Address:
   Phone:
3. Working Contact Person:
   Address:
   Phone:
4. Topic:
   Title:
5. Who will attend?
   How many will attend?
   Will they attend by choice or obligation?
   How much do they know about the topic?
   Why are they interested in this topic?
   Do they want an overview or specific information?
   How does this presentation relate to the rest of the inservice?
6. Location:
   Directions/Parking:
   Room Description:
   Microphone:
   Audio-visuals:
   Handouts:
   Miscellaneous:
7. Content Ideas Discussed:
8. Speaker will supply:
9. Sponsors will supply:

SAMPLE

PRESENTATION PLANNING GUIDE

Topic: How to serve deaf-blind students in the rhythm room. Explain music therapy.

Title: Music Therapy with the Deaf-blind

Objectives/Purposes You Want to State and Achieve:

1. Staff will understand the types of goals/objectives that will be generalized from the classroom/dorm instruction to the rhythm room.
2. Staff will be exposed to basic information about music therapy that directly relates to deaf-blind.

Critical Concepts You Want to Imply:

1. Music/rhythm room activities are fun for our deaf-blind students. (via videotape of actual students)
2. Remind staff of basic "human-ness" of students. (via activity on empathy)

Knowledge/Theoretical Base:

Definition of music therapy. Music therapy theory of finding pleasure within the environment, self, and with others. Discuss how that relates specifically to our students (self-stim, functioning levels of students), social relationships/interactions of students).
Videotape of students in music therapy. Activity for relaxation (after a day of teaching and students).

Activities for Presentation:	Equipment Needed:
1. Introduction: State objectives of workshop. Explain my work experience. Explain why and how the m.t. program was set up here.	
2. Guided imagery activity with activities for relaxation and empathy with objects.	Activity packet & equipment listed
3. Transition to empathy with students	
4. Discussion of m.t. theory and application of theory to our students.	chalkboard
5. Staff picks a student and applies the theory to the student. List the basic needs/desires that the student would name if they were able.	chalkboard
6. Point out how each of the basic needs is addressed through music therapy.	
7. Watch videotape. Point out goals/objectives being addressed.	VCR equipment
8. Closure and evaluation.	Evaluation forms

Dates Presented and to Whom: TSB/DB teaching staff 9/82
TSB/DB dorm staff 10/83

SAMPLE

NON-MUSIC INTERACTION ACTIVITY

Participants sketch a profile of a face on a blank sheet of paper. This should require only a few minutes.

Participants then divide the profile into six sections and number the sections one through six.

Participants answer six non-threatening personal questions. Questions, listing statements, and fill-in the blanks such as the following are most effective.

1. List three things your family enjoys doing together.
2. What is your all-time favorite book?
3. Name your favorite sport.
4. When I grow up, I would like to be a ________.
5. The thing I like best about a job is ________.
6. I was born in ________.
7. My pet peeve is ________.
8. My greatest ambition is to ________.
9. What was your favorite teacher like?
10. I admire parents because ________.
11. My birthday is ________.
12. My fantasy is to travel to ________.

The presenter collects the profiles, mixes them up, and redistributes them.

Each individual locates the owner of the profile and talks with them for a few minutes.

Each participant introduces the owner of their profile and states one or two facts about them.

Source: Strategies for Effective Parent-Teacher Interaction, A Guide for Teacher Trainers. Page 242-243. For information contact: Roger Kroth, Department of Special Education, University of New Mexico, Albuquerque, New Mexico.

HANDICAP RANKING SCALE

_________ Elementary Type of Handicap Taught _____________

_________ Secondary Sex: Male _________ Female _________

Categories of handicapping conditions are listed below. Please rank these, from one to ten, according to your own feelings, on the basis of severity. Which handicap do you feel is the most severe problem a child could have? Which handicap do you feel is second most serious? Which do you feel is the third most serious, and so forth. Consider only the individual and his problem in adjustment to school, community, and life.

Handicap	Rank
1. Blindness	____
2. Brain injury	____
3. Crippled and other health impaired	____
4. Deafness and hearing impairment	____
5. Emotional Disturbance	____
6. Epilepsy	____
7. Gifted	____
8. Learning Disabilities	____
9. Mental Retardation	____
10. Speech Impaired	____

Source: Kroth, Roger L. and Simpson, Richard L. <u>Parent Conferences as a Teaching Strategy</u>. Denver, CO: Love Publishing Company, 1977.

OUTLINE HANDOUT

Note: A handout in outline form gives the participant space to write down notes about major points covered in the presentation.

MUSIC THERAPY IN NURSING HOMES

I. GOALS OF A MUSIC PROGRAM IN A NURSING HOME

1. To increase SOCIALIZATION and PARTICIPATION
2. To encourage SELF-HELP SKILLS
3. To encourage POSITIVE ATTITUDES
4. To improve SELF-ESTEEM and SELF-CONFIDENCE
5. To encourage REALITY ORIENTATION
6. To provide opportunities for EXERCISE

II. IDEAS FOR MUSIC ACTIVITIES

1. MUSIC CLUB (music listening, field trips, coordinate special music)
2. SPECIAL OCCASION SINGERS (sing for parties, guest performers, serenades)
3. RHYTHM BAND (make instruments, ensemble, special performance)
4. GUEST PERFORMERS
5. MUSICAL EXERCISE (for general fitness or specific conditions)
6. MUSIC LESSONS FOR CLIENTS (group or private lessons)

III. MUSIC THERAPY

A music therapist uses music as a tool to help clients reach specific target objectives. For example, a music therapist might work with clients who display inappropriate behaviors such as hostility toward others, poor personal grooming, or unusual mannerisms.

NARRATIVE HANDOUT

Note: A narrative handout might include general background information about music therapy as well as brief samples of goals, objectives, and activities and a bibliography of resources and materials.

MUSIC THERAPY

Music therapy is the prescribed use of music and music related activities to modify ineffective learning patterns, influence changes in behavior, and develop non-music goals.

Job opportunities for music therapists are in clinical, educational, and private settings where there are children or adults who require special services because of mental, behavioral, learning, or physical disorders. Clients/students vary in age and degree of handicap from the deaf infant to the schizophrenic child to the geriatric patient whose difficulties are due to aging. Facilities include, but are not limited to, public school systems, medical and psychiatric hospitals and clinics, rehabilitation centers, correctional institutions, and geriatric programs.

In order to fully understand music therapy, it is necessary to discuss three basic concepts of music as it relates to the individual. First, music permeates culture and has since the beginning of man. Society instinctively sings, listens, dances, and moves to music. From singing in the shower to tapping feet, people respond to music.

WORKSHEET HANDOUT

Note: A worksheet may be used separately or in conjunction with an outline or narrative handout. It is completed by the participants at the presenter's direction during a specified portion of the workshop.

Adaptive P. E.	Art therapy	Dance therapy	Music therapy	Occupational therapy	Orientation & mobility	Physical therapy	Speech therapy	SUPPORT SERVICES: HOW DO THEY RELATE?
								Service Descriptions
								Direct, individual in a clinical setting
								Direct, individual in a classroom setting
								Direct, group (2 or more clients) in a clinical setting
								Direct, group (2 or more students) in the classroom
								Combination of direct and consultation
								Ongoing consultation with direct care providers for clients/students
								Consultation with parents
								Consultation with other specialists
								Other:

Adaptive physical education and mainstreamed physical education:

Music therapy and mainstreamed music education:

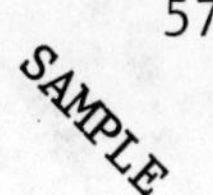

Presentation Evaluation

1. The content of the workshop met my expectations.

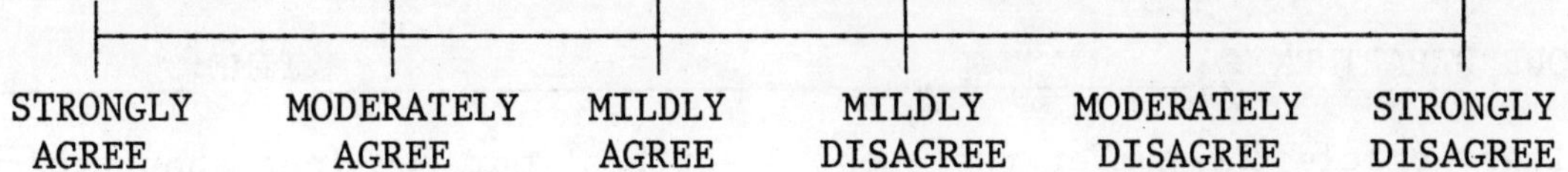

STRONGLY AGREE | MODERATELY AGREE | MILDLY AGREE | MILDLY DISAGREE | MODERATELY DISAGREE | STRONGLY DISAGREE

2. The instructors seemed knowledgeable about the topics presented.

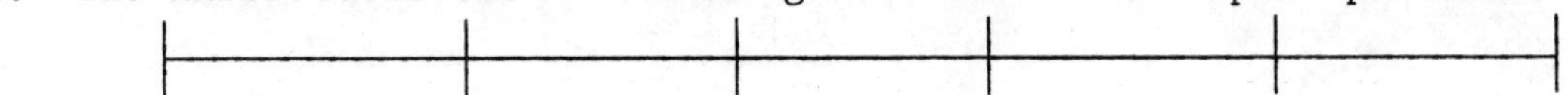

3. The experiential portions of the workshop seemed relevant and effective.

4. The material presented will be useful to me in my job setting.

5. I would recommend this workshop to others.

6. Audiovisual aids were used effectively in this workshop.

7. Handouts and printed material were useful.

8. The workshop seemed well-paced.

9. The aspect(s) of the presentation most useful to me is (are):

10. I would recommend the following changes in the presentation:

11. Comments:

(use the back of this sheet, if necessary)

SAMPLE

WORKSHOP FEEDBACK FORM

WORKSHOP/PRESENTOR:________________________ DATE:__________

YOUR DEPARTMENT:________________________ TIME:__________

Please circle the number that best describes your feelings about the workshop.

	Not at all		Somewhat		Very much so
1. Were the objectives of the workshop achieved?	0	1	2	3	4
2. Was the organization and presentation of the workshop well done?	0	1	2	3	4
3. How useful was the content of the workshop to you?	0	1	2	3	4
4. Was the presentor a skillful speaker?	0	1	2	3	4
5. Was the presentor an expert on the topic?	0	1	2	3	4
6. Would you like more or continued training on this topic?	0	1	2	3	4
7. Would you recommend this workshop to others?	0	1	2	3	4

Comments/suggestions (Use back if necessary):

* Most valuable part of the workshop?____________________

____

* Least valuable part of the workshop?____________________

____

* Related topics you would like information on?____________________

____

SAMPLE

PRESENTATION EVALUATION

QUESTIONS	RATING SCALE: Excellent	GOOD	FAIR	POOR	COMMENTS
1. Goals of the workshop					
2. Content					
3. Relevance of the information to your job setting.					
4. Handouts					
5. Organization and presentation.					

General Comments:

Financial considerations arise for music therapists who work for agencies as well as for those who are self-employed. Developing good business sense is critical for music therapists. Cost-effective programs and fiscally responsible employees receive administrative endorsement and agency support even in periods of budget cuts.

FINANCIAL PLANNING

Taking responsibility for financial matters requires being informed, setting goals, developing and maintaining a budget, and keeping careful records. The key to good money management is approaching personal and professional finances in a systematic, business-like manner.

Numerous books, periodicals, and seminars provide information about money management. Professionals in banking, accounting, and investment counseling can give advice on various money matters. Seek advice from financial experts and remain aware of financial trends, then use common sense when taking charge of finances.

Define professional and personal financial goals and review them regularly. Clarify values and spending habits, then set ambitious yet realistic short-term and long-term goals including provisions for a savings plan, an emergency fund, and money for regular living expenses.

A budget includes projected income as well as expenditures. Analyze current spending habits by writing down every expense for a month, then multiply by twelve to estimate total expenses for a year at current spending levels. Another budget analysis method is to categorize all expenditures from the previous year and project expenses in those categories for the coming year. Samples of budget analysis worksheets are located on pages 73 and 74.

Once past spending patterns are analyzed, one can check financial goals, make adjustments in budget categories as needed, then write a projected monthly budget, balancing income, expenditures, and spending habits. A sample budget form is on page 75.

Keep careful records of projected and annual income and expenses. Other financial records should be kept in a safe, accessible file. Some records are best kept in a safe-deposit box, while others belong in home or business files. Refer to the "Personal Financial Records" on page 76 for suggestions.

NEGOTIATING A FAIR SALARY

The music therapist should evaluate several points before determining salary or professional fees. First, expertise is valuable. Consider the amount and kinds of education, job experiences, and any other special skills one has that will benefit the agency and its clientele. Second, time is valuable. Time spent in service delivery, planning and preparation, conferences, staffings, and other job-related tasks should be adequately compensated for by the professional fee or salary. Last, job-related expenses warrant consideration. A therapist working on an agency's staff should consider job-related costs such as transportation, child care, clothing, professional dues, and pre-employment expenses before accepting a salary. A self-employed therapist will have those considerations as well as office expenses, insurance, and other overhead costs that will affect the contract rate.

When seeking a job with an agency or developing a private practice, music therapists invest time and money. Time spent contacting administrators, presenting workshops, and preparing written materials is unpaid time. The amount of investment capital required depends upon the nature of the program the music therapist wishes to develop. Expenses that frequently arise include office supplies, postage, printing, advertising, basic supplies and materials, and transportation costs. A salary or contract rate should be adequate to compensate the therapist for these pre-employment expenses.

In negotiating a salary or raise, remember that income may be in actual salary or contract rate or in fringe benefits. A wide range of possibilities for salary improvement are available through fringe benefits. Negotiations might include:

- Availability of a secretary, computer, copy machine, video equipment, or other equipment
- Equipment and supplies provided by the agency
- Increased vacation time
- Paid sick days
- Planning and/or reporting periods
- Professional growth conferences or workshops (expenses, paid leave time)
- Shorter working days or years
- Transportation time and/or mileage

Increasing fees or obtaining a raise requires assertiveness. If a raise is immediately unobtainable, a six-month review will provide the employee an opportunity for future negotiations and the employer time to evaluate the situation. It is helpful to maintain professional relationships with other persons in social service positions in order to remain up-to-date on actual salaries and contract fees applicable to music therapists.

In determining prices for private individuals or groups, consider not only direct service time, but also time spent in preparation, documentation, and consultation. Service prices should be reasonable for families of handicapped individuals. Cohesive therapy groups with reduced rates are more profitable for the therapist and more affordable for clients. Competitive, fair prices that adequately cover professional services and overhead costs are important for current and future career success.

MAINTAINING A COST-EFFECTIVE PROGRAM

The following guidelines are helpful in developing goals that result in a cost-effective music therapy program:

- Be accountable. Document the program plan and client progress.
- Be visible to agency staff and administration.
- Budget carefully for expenses such as music instruments, equipment, supplies, and materials. Prioritize the need for various items and remain cognizant of program expenses.
- Continually evaluate the quality of the program. Introduce new techniques and improvements whenever possible.
- Demonstrate fiscal responsibility.
- Develop documentation that demonstrates cost-effectiveness. Provide these reports to administrators and other agency personnel.
- Increase overall awareness of the value of the music therapy program.
- Present a positive, professional image.
- Take advantage of professional growth experiences to assure up-to-date techniques and services.
- Work hard with energy and enthusiasm.

SELF-EMPLOYMENT

The principles involved in financial planning, negotiating a fair salary, and maintaining a cost-effective program apply to music therapists regardless of their type of employment. However, self-employed music therapists have additional financial considerations. The Small Business Administration, bankers, accountants, lawyers, and insurance professionals are good sources of information about investment capital, record keeping, taxes, and other legal and financial concerns.

Getting Started Financially

A major consideration for self-employed music therapists is supplementary income while the business is developing. If the therapist is married, and the spouse earns enough to support the family, a supplementary income may not be as crucial as for those who provide the sole financial support of a family. During this period of job development, time for exploring the market is essential. Any commitment to a part-time job must be carefully balanced with marketing time. An ideal part-time job is one involving work with potential clients or agencies such as being an aid or substitute in public or private school special education classes, a sheltered workshop, a half-way house, or rehabilitation facilities. Another option is teaching private students (normal or handicapped). However, this too requires marketing a skill. Private music teachers will make referrals of handicapped students for music instruction if they are aware of the availability of music therapy services in the community.

Some investment capital is necessary when starting a music therapy practice, just as in any business. Some expenses to anticipate are:

- Advertising
- Child care
- Insurance
- Legal advice
- Marketing materials
- Music and other materials
- Musical instruments
- Office space
- Office supplies and equipment
- Postage
- Telephone/answering machine
- Transportation

A key to a successful start is keeping overhead expenses to a minimum, adding extra equipment and supplies as program expansion increases income.

Small business experts advise setting aside ten percent of gross earnings in interest-bearing accounts to be used only for paying insurance premiums and benefits such as sick days and vacation leave. Another ten percent of gross income should be reserved for reinvesting in the business. In the case of a music therapist, this might involve supplies, equipment, materials, advertising, insurance, and professional growth. The percentage of gross income that is reserved for paying taxes will depend upon one's tax bracket. After a regular monthly salary is withdrawn, any excess income should be invested.

Keeping Records

Although accurate records of business transactions are important for all working people, they are critical for the self-employed. Computerized bookkeeping systems are helpful and may save time. If a computer is not available, a system that can be used includes a running balance sheet, an itemized record of all income and expenditures, copies of all statements sent for professional services rendered, and categorized files of expenditures for tax purposes.

Sample Balance Sheet

	September	Receipts	Disbursements	Balance
9/12	(906) Southwest Music		23.58	798.73
9/15	Deposit	578.00		1376.73
9/18	(907) City Office Supply		5.79	1370.94

Sample Income Itemization

	September	payment	balance
9/06	Michael Jones (private)	23.00	23.00
9/06	Sandy Lee (private)	20.00	43.00
9/07	Sunny Ridge School	360.00	403.00

Sample monthly statements for an agency and for private clients are found at the end of this chapter. A separate business checking account is an option that allows for accurate, up-to-date records of all business income and expenditures. In most cases, checks are adequate receipts for tax purposes.

Taxes

The Internal Revenue Service (IRS) publishes comprehensive booklets and guidelines for self-employed persons. Since tax rules do change frequently, it is always wise to verify tax regulations each year. Deductions that self-employed individuals should investigate include:

- Advertising
- Car expense
- Depreciation
- Donations
- Insurance
- Interest
- Legal and professional service fees
- Music supplies

- Office supplies
- Postage
- Professional dues and publications
- Rent and utilities
- Repairs
- Taxes
- Telephone
- Travel and entertainment

Canceled checks or receipts should be filed in appropriate categories at the end of each month. Although salaried employees can legally deduct fewer expenses, tax deductions should be investigated. Professional and/or business expenses not reimbursed by the agency are usually tax deductible. Such expenses may include travel, room and board for professional trips, professional books, materials, equipment, certain educational expenses, and child care expenses incurred because of work and work-related obligations.

Self-employed music therapists may consider hiring a Certified Public Accountant (CPA) to prepare their tax return. In many cases, the money saved by the CPA's specialized knowledge is a far greater amount than the money spent for services. The CPA may also provide excellent suggestions on actions to take during the coming year to protect income and to improve financial management skills.

FINAL NOTE

Music therapy is a service-based profession, making cost-effectiveness more difficult to prove than in a retail situation. Therefore, therapists must develop business skills so their programs survive in a financially motivated society. As the availability of social service funds ride the financial roller coaster, music therapists should continue to seek new and creative ways to earn income and manage money more efficiently.

SUGGESTIONS FOR FURTHER READING

Behr, M. & Lazar, W. (1983). Women working home: The home-based business guide and directory (2nd ed.). Edison, NJ: Women Working Home Press.

Conn, C.P. (1981). Making it happen. Old Tappen, NJ: Fleming H. Revell Company.

Davis, M. (Speaker). (1985). The profit prescription: A guide to management before crisis. (Cassette Tape Series). Chicago, IL: Nightingale-Conant Corporation.

Feldman Neuer, B. (1983). Homebased businesses (3rd ed.). Los Angeles, CA: Till Press.

Hewes, J.J. (1981). Worksteads. New York, NY: Dolphin Books/Doubleday.

Kamaroff, B. (1981). Small time operator (Revised ed.). Laytonville, CA: Bell Springs Publishers.

Lowry, A.J. (1981). How to become financially successful by owning your own business. New York, NY: Simon & Schuster.

Porter, S. (1979). Sylvia Porter's new money book for the 80's. Garden City, NY: Doubleday & Co., Inc.

Quinn, J.B. (1979). Everyone's money book. New York, NY: Delacorte Press.

Schuller, R.H. & Dunn, P.D. (1985). The power of being debt free. Nashville, TN: Thomas Nelson, Inc.

Van Caspel, V. (1983). The power of money dynamics. Reston, VA: Reston Publishing Company, Inc.

Winston, S. (1979). The entrepreneurial woman. New York, NY: Newsweek Books and Bantam Books.

SAMPLE

BUDGET ANALYSIS WORKSHEET
(A - B = $ for C)

A. INCOME:	TOTAL PREVIOUS YEAR	PROJECTED TOTAL CURRENT YEAR	ACTUAL TOTAL CURRENT YEAR
Salary			
Dividends/Interest			
Other			
TOTAL			
B. NECESSARY EXPENDITURES:			
Car maintenance/repair			
Child care			
Clothing			
Contributions			
Credit cards/charges			
Education			
Food			
Gifts			
Health care (Doctor, dentist, drugs)			
Housing maintenance/repair			
Insurance premiums			
Investments			
Loans			
Personal allowance/care			
Phone			
Professional dues, subscriptions			
Professional services			
Rent/mortgage			
Savings			
Taxes			
Transportation			
Utilities			
TOTAL			
C. NON-ESSENTIAL ITEMS			
Entertainment			
Travel/vacation			
Furniture/household help			
Other			
TOTAL			

ANALYZING THE BUDGET

Never plan a budget during a financial panic. Be in a neutral frame-of-mind. Remember: a budget that conflicts with spending habits will not work.

1. To determine spending habits, keep a diary of expenditures for at least two weeks and preferably for one month. List every item and its cost to you. At the end of the recording period make a total for each category of expenditures. Based upon the actual spending habits, determine financial priorities and limits.

2. List all expenditures you cannot change without making major changes in your lifestyle.

   Housing: Rent/mortgage ________
   Utilities (gas, water, phone, electricity) ________
   Other (cleaning, gardner, etc.) ________
   Food: ________
   Automobile expense/maintenance: ________
   Medical and dental expense: ________
   Insurance: Health ________
   Life ________
   Homeowner's or renter's ________
   Personal property ________
   Automobile ________
   Other ________
   Loans: Installment ________
   Charge accounts ________
   Other ________
   Taxes: ________
   Professional expenses: Membership dues ________
   Publications ________
   Allowance for yourself: ________
   Other (child care): ________
   TOTAL EXPENSES ________

3. Make a list of irregular, but necessary expenses:

   Housing maintenance and repair: ________
   Car repair: ________
   Medical bills: ________
   Contributions, Tithes: ________
   Gifts: ________
   Other (investments, savings plan): ________
   TOTAL EXPENSES ________

4. List pleasure items:

   Classes and lessons: ________
   Clothing: ________
   Entertainment: ________
   Furniture: ________
   Vacations: ________
   Other: ________
   TOTAL EXPENSES ________

COMBINE TOTALS OF 2, 3, AND 4. THE TOTAL EQUALS HOW MUCH INCOME YOU MUST EARN IN ORDER TO NOT CHANGE YOUR LIFESTYLE OR GO INTO DEBT.

MONTHLY BUDGET SHEET
FOR THE MONTH OF

____

INCOME	BUDGETED	ACTUAL	DIFFERENCE
Earned income (salary)			
Investment income			
Other income			
TOTAL INCOME			

EXPENDITURES	BUDGETED	ACTUAL	DIFFERENCE
Fixed Expenses			
Automobile insurance			
Automobile loan			
Child care			
Contributions			
Emergency fund			
Homeowner's or renter's insurance			
Medical/life insurance			
Other loans (including credit cards)			
Professional fees			
Rent/mortgage			
Savings/investment			
Taxes (property, income)			
Other			
Flexible Expenses			
Automobile repair			
Clothing/personal care			
Entertainment			
Furniture			
Gifts			
Groceries			
Household maintenance			
Medical			
Telephone			
Transportation			
Utilities			
Other			
TOTAL EXPENSES			

TOTAL INCOME: ______________

MINUS TOTAL EXPENSES: ______________

EQUALS BALANCE ______________

SAMPLE

PERSONAL FINANCIAL RECORDS

Attorney, accountant, executor, trustees: name, address, phone number

Brokerage accounts: name of broker, address, account numbers

Checking and savings accounts: name of bank, address, account number, location of bankbook or checkbook

Credit cards: company name, card number, phone number for reporting lost cards

Current taxes: cancelled checks and receipts for deductibles, income receipts, records of capital gains and losses, quarterly estimated tax forms

Employee benefits: description, location of benefit statements, person to contact at company

Hard assets (precious metals, gems, collectibles): type, quality, quantity, purchase date, gross price, date sold, net proceeds, location of maintenance and tax receipts, storage location, tax forms, and income records

Keogh plans and IRAs: location of investment, address, account number

Letter of instructions in case of death: location

Life insurance policies: company, amount, beneficiaries, policy number, location of policy

Money market funds: name of fund, address, phone number, account number location of statements

Net worth statement: latest annual appraisal of assets and liabilities

Real estate deeds: address of property, register number, location of papers

Real estate investments: type of property, address, purchase date, gross price, depreciation schedule, when sold, net proceeds, location of maintenance and tax receipts, tax forms and income records

Safe deposit box: location, number, where inventory of contents and key are stored

Securities: name, number of shares and units, serial numbers, purchase date, gross price, sale date, net proceeds, where certificates and transactions slips are located

Stockbroker, insurance agent: name, address, phone

Tax records: location of all returns, schedules and documentation for the previous years

Time deposits: name of bank, address, principal, interest rate, maturity date, account number, location of certificate or bankbook

Wills and trusts: locations of originals and copies

Once employed, the music therapist must be aware of a number of procedures and processes in one's daily work. Because keeping a job is as important as getting a job, the therapist should make every effort to provide quality services and to be a valuable employee, contractual consultant, or private therapist. The process begins with clarifying responsibilities of all parties involved and ends with periodic evaluation of all aspects of service delivery.

DEFINITION OF JOB RESPONSIBILITIES

Most agencies have written job descriptions for their staff. The music therapist should review the job description with the supervisor, asking for clarification if needed.

The policies and procedures of an agency will, of course, affect the music therapist. It is important to become acquainted with these and to adhere to them closely. Policies and procedures usually cover the responsibilities of the agency and its employees as well as guidelines concerning client behavior. The following points may be included in an agency's official policies and procedures:

- Agency structure
- Amenities (dress codes, administrative courtesies)
- Client eligibility criteria and priorities for services
- Inservice training and workshops
- Provision of services (philosophy)
- Referral process
- Roles of the personnel participating in the program
- Specific guidelines for client discipline, client rights, and complaint procedures
- Specific services provided

A self-employed music therapist needs a contract with each agency. A contract should include: the name of the contracting agency and the contracted therapist, the amount of time contracted, the fee and method of payment, the clients or personnel served, and the responsibilities of administrators, supervisors, direct care providers, and the music therapist. Other points that might be included in a contract or in a supplementary written agreement are:

- Budget for materials and supplies
- Client eligibility criteria
- Policies about access to agency supplies and materials, office equipment, and office personnel
- Procedures for program evaluation and contract renewal
- Procedures for referral, assessment, documentation, progress reporting

Pages 91 through 93 contain several samples of contracts and responsibility summaries.

PROTECTION

Music therapists should take all necessary steps to protect themselves, their clients, and their equipment and office space. For their own protection, music therapists often investigate liability and malpractice insurance. It is important to maintain accurate up-to-date documentation of all aspects of work, and to keep current copies of release forms on file. Self-employed music therapists might consider health, life, and disability insurance. Most agencies require such policies for their on-staff personnel. Music therapists should be aware of copyright laws and regulations when copying music or using materials for public performance.

Arrange equipment and furnishings in rooms for music therapy sessions to prevent accidents. The therapist may have to request barrier-free access. In case an accident does occur, the therapist should have a working knowledge of first-aid and CPR. Emergency telephone numbers and access to assistance should be readily available.

Safeguarding equipment and office space involves installing additional security (dead-bolt locks, burglar alarms, outside lights) if necessary, keeping records of all serial numbers on all equipment, and installing smoke detectors in the office and storage areas. Confirm that the space and equipment is adequately covered by insurance. Investigate service agreements for mechanical equipment and learn minor equipment repair and maintenance procedures.

DOCUMENTATION

Documentation of each phase of service delivery must be concise and reliable to be useful to the therapist and other professionals who utilize the information. Besides being legally binding and protective, accurate documentation can also help to demonstrate the cost-effectiveness of a program to administrators. Well-written reports and forms communicate the validity of the music therapy program to others.

Clear, concise forms minimize the time spent by the therapist on required paperwork. Forms should record pertinent information about the client and allow for valid interpretation of that information. An up-to-date filing system makes all documentation easily accessible.

Many agencies will have required documentation forms. If necessary, the therapist may want to develop supplementary forms that will provide more complete program information. Numerous samples of forms used in referrals, assessments, treatment plans, program planning, progress notes, and progress reports are located at the end of this chapter.

Confidentiality of records and client anonymity is important. Many agencies require that all records be kept in a locked area and seen only by approved professionals. Written permission is usually necessary for the use of any client photograph or film. Deletion of personally identifiable information (such as the name of the client or client's family, social security number, list of characteristics, or other information that would make identification possible with reasonable certainty) is essential when showing documents to unapproved personnel.

SCHEDULING

Scheduling is often the most difficult part of a music therapist's job. The client may have classes, therapy sessions, a work schedule, strict feeding or medication times, or other commitments limiting the choice of times for music therapy. The scheduled therapy times must meet the needs of the client, music therapist, and agency. It is important to work closely with other direct care providers in a spirit of cooperation and compromise when scheduling music therapy sessions.

Unfortunately, many agencies fully expect the music therapy department (whether staffed by one person or ten) to service an incredible number of clients. Negotiation is a viable tool in such a situation. Provide progress records, data, and any other pertinent information helpful to support the need for small numbers. Group therapy sessions are only beneficial for clients with similar goals. The client's need for group experiences should be the main consideration. Negotiation includes compromise, so be ready to give something in return. There are times and places that negotiation and compromise cannot change the present situation in any way. In such a case, carry on the best way possible. Keep close records and plan to try for negotiation again when the time seems right.

A self-employed music therapist may find the need to schedule after school hours or after work hours if contracting with the client or client's family directly. Evenings and/or weekends are always alternative time slots, but consider trading that time elsewhere; e.g., if working weekends, take a "weekend" off somewhere during the week.

These sample schedules pertain to agency employment for direct services, agency employment for consultative services, and self-employment.

Agency Employment for Direct Services

Monday	Tuesday	Wednesday	Thursday	Friday
8:00-11:30 Clients 12:00-1:00 Lunch 1:00-3:00 Office 3:30-5:00 Clients	8:00-11:30 Clients 12:00-1:00 Lunch 1:00-3:00 Office 3:30-5:00 Clients	8:00-11:30 Clients 12:00-1:00 Lunch 1:00-3:00 Office 3:30-5:00 Clients	8:00-11:30 Clients 12:00-1:00 Lunch 1:00-3:00 Office 3:30-5:00 Clients	8:00-11:30 Clients 12:00-1:00 Lunch 1:00-4:30 Staffing

Agency Employment for Consultative Services

Monday	Tuesday	Wednesday	Thursday	Friday
8:00-11:30 Demon. to personnel 2:00-5:00 Inservice	8:00-11:30 Demon. and discussion with pers.	8:00-11:30 Demon. and discussion with pers.	8:00-11:30 Planning and Docum. (in office)	8:00-11:30 Review and observation with personnel

Self-Employment
Direct and Consultative Services

Monday	Tuesday	Wednesday	Thursday	Friday
	9:00-2:15 public school special educ. program	10:00-1:00 Office	8:00-11:00 Intermediate Care Facilities for the Mentally Retarded	
2:00-6:00 Foster care facility	3:00-6:00 Private clients	1:30-6:30 Private clients (individuals and groups)	11:30-3:30 Public school special educ. program	

PROCEDURAL GUIDELINES

Each agency will vary somewhat in its procedures for service delivery. Some agencies have flowcharts or other guidelines. In many cases, the music therapist will need to develop a specific step-by-step method for working with clients. Steps for providing direct care to clients include:

- Referral
- Assessment
- Recommendations for services
- Treatment plan
- Therapy sessions
- Data collection
- Verbal and written progress reports
- On-going Consultation
- Termination of services

If the agency does not have written procedural guidelines specific to music therapy, the therapist might provide written copies to administrators, supervisors, and direct care staff. Awareness of the inner workings of a program leads to staff cooperation, smooth operation, and support.

THERAPY TECHNIQUES

Familiarity with many aspects of music and therapeutic styles and techniques helps therapists provide programming that best meets each client's needs. Specialization in certain populations or techniques allows a music therapist to develop more concentrated expertise.

National and regional organizations such as the National Piano Foundation and the Music Educator's National Conference as well as music stores and catalogues are valuable resources for locating teaching materials. Because a client's program may include music materials from a variety of sources, a pocketed folder or notebook to organize all materials is often useful. The self-responsibility of bringing the folder to music therapy is a good habit for clients to develop.

PROFESSIONALISM

When working with people in a professional capacity, sincere interest and concern, as well as listening in an open, non-judgmental manner, are important. Open communication and cooperation with co-workers help everyone develop programs most beneficial to clients and staff. Each party must accept full responsibility for communicating clearly.

Avoid negative influences, complainers, and office squabbles when possible. Dealing with solutions and alternatives is more constructive than concentrating on problems. When difficult problems are encountered, document details, report specific facts, and suggest specific solutions. Report concerns through the appropriate channels as stated in the agency's policies and procedures guidelines. When responsible for a problem, do not dwell on the mistake, but move to rectify the situation quickly.

A positive professional image is portrayed by a person who understands his job and does it well. Some characteristics of successful professionals include:

- Cooperation with others: acknowledge help from others, and communicate openly.
- Dependability: accept responsibility and follow through with tasks.
- Positive attitude: have faith in yourself and concentrate on the positive aspects of your work.
- Self-motivation: anticipate what needs to be done and do it.
- Superior performance: develop discipline and challenge yourself.

Professional credibility is often associated with one's personal appearance. Dressing with authority is helpful in establishing a professional image at an inservice workshop or job interview. On the other hand, it is more practical to dress informally when working with youngsters on gross motor tasks. A neat appearance and comfortable, sensible clothing leave a positive impression on others.

SERVING PRIVATE CLIENTS

Although one of the advantages of contracting services is that the therapist's schedule allows time for working with private clients, the on-staff employee may choose this option too. Important points to consider are obtaining clients, locating an area for therapy sessions, maintaining a professional image, and providing services for individuals rather than agencies.

In order to obtain clients, the music therapist must take advantage of all opportunities for publicity, as confidentiality of records makes obtaining clients difficult. In some cases, advertising is appropriate and effective. Making presentations to various organizations such as the local chapter of the Music Teacher's National Association or parent support groups are ways of increasing awareness of available services. Contacting private psychologists or psychiatrists may result in referrals. Some agencies will send information about the music therapy program home with clients.

Therapy sessions can be held in a rented space or in a home studio. In any case, the area must be private, pleasant, and conducive to therapy. If the sessions are held in your home, family needs and schedules must also be considered. An ideal situation is having a therapy room with an outside entrance that is removed from the living area of your home. Locating an affordable and appropriate area for therapy outside the home may be difficult. Churches, pre-schools, or agencies that serve handicapped individuals may exchange room space for weekly music sessions with their students or clients.

A unique characteristic of working with private clients is that the music therapist is responsible directly to the client and family members rather than to an agency. The music therapist will therefore want to work closely with the client or the client's family or guardians in the following areas:

- Developing procedures to be used at home that will reinforce target skills.
- Establishing short-term and long-term goals and objectives.
- Obtaining relevant background information on the client.
- Providing the family information to assist them in obtaining music therapy services through agencies serving the client or reimbursements for services via third party payments.

Annual planning conferences (similar to an agency's interdisciplinary team meeting), informal discussions at the end of therapy sessions, brief progress memos, and telephone conversations are useful in maintaining open communication. Families of handicapped individuals are experiencing unique life situations. Therefore, the music therapist should be empathetic, non-judgmental, non-threatening, and a good listener.

Parents or guardians may request written information from the music therapist for use by other professionals working with the client. These program plans, evaluations, and progress reports will make an impression upon doctors, counselors, direct care providers, social workers, and/or administrators and can assist the music therapist in obtaining future referrals as these professionals become aware of the music therapy program.

FINAL NOTE

Periodically evaluate all job procedures. When needed, make adjustments that improve the quality of your services or of the general program. Approach the job from a new angle or different attitude. Changing music therapy planning or documentation forms may help the music therapist create new interest in the program.

SUGGESTIONS FOR FURTHER READING

Austin, R.W. Fair use copying for the classroom. Portland, ME: J. Weston Walch, Publisher.

Bastien, J.W. (1977). How to teach piano successfully (2nd ed.). San Diego, CA: Neil A. Kjos Music Company.

Scott, Foresman, & Company. The new copyright law. Glenview, IL: Author.

Vernazza, M. Piano in the Education of the Handicapped Child. (Brochure). Dallas, TX: National Piano Foundation.

SAMPLE FORMAT

CONTRACT FOR MUSIC THERAPY SERVICES

1. Contracting Agency
   Address
   Contact Person

2. Contracted Music Therapist
   Address
   Registration Number

3. Responsibilities of Contracting Agency

4. Responsibilities of Administrators/Supervisors

5. Responsibilities of Direct Care Providers

6. Responsibilities of Music Therapist

7. Clients/Personnel/Agencies Served

8. Hours/Days/Weeks Contracted

9. Fee/Method of Payment

____________________ ______________________________

Date Authorizing Administrator

____

Music Therapist

SUMMARY OF

CONTRACTUAL MUSIC THERAPY SERVICES

Therapist's name
Address
Telephone

RESPONSIBILITIES OF THE SPONSORING AGENCY

1. To provide funding for the music therapy program (a monthly statement will be sent by the therapist).
2. To provide guidelines to the therapist concerning scheduling, referral procedures, documentation requirements, relevant agency policies, etc.
3. To provide an area for therapy sessions.
4. To provide access to copy machine and secretary.

RESPONSIBILITIES OF COOPERATING AGENCY

1. To refer clients to program and complete referral checklist.
2. To consult with the therapist about special needs of clients, scheduling, and client progress.

RESPONSIBILITIES OF THE MUSIC THERAPIST

1. To provide supplies (paper, pens, pencils, stickers, etc.) and equipment (guitar, rhythm instruments, tape recorders, etc.).
2. To provide transportation time and costs.
3. To present inservice or information sessions for participating staff, parents, and other personnel as requested.
4. To assist staff in referrals as requested.
5. To assess clients referred to the program.
6. To define target objectives and goals for each client.
7. To develop programs and procedures for each client.
8. To provide direct service to clients on a weekly basis.
9. To document progress of each client.
10. To regularly report progress to staff.
11. To consult with treatment team members as requested.

FEES

The fee for professional services is $__________ per direct service hour. The therapist does not charge for sick days, agency holidays, insurance, retirement, or other fringe benefits.

SAMPLE

CONTRACTUAL MUSIC THERAPY SERVICES
SUMMARY OF RESPONSIBILITIES

Administrator:____

- Completes a contract with the music therapist
- Reimburses music therapist once a month at the rate of $________ per direct service hour

Principal:____

- Verifies direct service hours provided by music therapist
- Provides space for music therapy sessions

Program Supervisor:____

- Refers students and teachers
- Informs the music therapist of relevant policies and procedures
- Acts as liaison in establishing, implementing, and maintaining music therapy services

Teacher:____

- Provides general programming information
- Observes and discusses the music therapy program
- Learns activities for own professional development

Music Therapist:____

- Evaluates students with regard to music therapy needs
- Designs goals, objectives, and activities for students
- Conducts regular music therapy sessions with students
- Reports progress of students to school personnel and parents
- Consults with school personnel and parents regarding the music therapy program
- Does not charge for: Equipment, materials, supplies
  Vacation and sick leave
  Health and life insurance
  Retirement program
  Program planning time (optional)
  Consultation time (within reason)
  Travel time (optional)
  Professional leave time (optional)
- Maintains classroom folders
- Provides documentation of music therapy services to administrators
- Presents inservice workshops as requested

SAMPLE

REFERRAL FOR MUSIC THERAPY

Name of Client:______________________________ Date:__________

Placement:__________________________________ D.O.B.:________

Team Leader:______________________________

Social Functioning Level:______________________________

Person(s) Making the Referral:__________________________

What is the observable behavior that you feel is interfering the most with this client's functioning?______________________________

____

What other therapies is this client receiving?____________________

Has this client received music therapy in the past?_____ If so, when?_____

What days and times would this client NOT be available for music therapy sessions?______________________________

____
Music Therapist

Treatment Suggestions:

____
Attending Psychiatrist

SAMPLE

SCREENING FOR MUSIC THERAPY

CLIENT ____________________ DIRECT CARE PROVIDER ____________________ LOCATION ____________________

PROBLEM AREAS	√	COMMENTS

Date of Screening ____________________

Completed by: Name
Music Therapist

MUSIC THERAPY

OBSERVATIONAL SCREENING TOOL

CIRCLE THOSE ITEMS THAT WOULD BEST IDENTIFY THE CLIENT YOU ARE REFERRING. ADD ANY ADDITIONAL COMMENTS IN THE MARGIN. <u>ALL</u> YOUR OBSERVATIONS ARE IMPORTANT.

I. ATTENTION SPAN:
- A. Easily distractible
- B. Does not remain in seat
- C. Cannot stand still
- D. Comments:

II. BEHAVIOR:
- A. Aggressive - Persecutor
- B. Withdrawn - Victim
- C. Excessively verbal
- D. Manipulative
- E. Comments:

III. ACADEMICS:
- A. Is performing on academic grade level
- B. Is not performing on academic grade level
- C. Non-graded program
- D. Comments:

IV. VISUAL-PERCEPTUAL:
- A. Places head very near objects
- B. Difficulty discriminating forms
- C. Immature or disjointed drawings of persons, geometrics
- D. Comments:

V. FINE MOTOR:
- A. Difficulty performing manipulative tasks (cutting with scissors, etc.)
- B. Difficulty grasping small objects
- C. Difficulty imitating fine motor movements
- D. Comments:

VI. GROSS MOTOR COORDINATION:
- A. Clumsy, falls or trips often
- B. Poor balance and/or equilibrium
- C. Poor body awareness
- D. Comments:

VII. OTHER:

______________________________	(Direct Care Provider) ______________________________
Client Referred	Referred By

____

Date

SAMPLE

MUSIC THERAPY REFERRAL

Teacher:________________________ Aide:________________________

Classroom:________________________ School:________________________

Number of Students:______________

Student	Disability	Grade	Age

Indicate students receiving the following services:

____Adaptive P.E.
____Audiological services
____Counseling
____Medical Diagnostic
____Music Education
____Music Therapy
____Occupational Therapy
____Orientation/Mobility
____Physical Education
____Physical Therapy
____Resource Room
____Speech Therapy
____Visual Training

Indicate which of the following is available:

____Record player
____Rhythm instruments
____Other:________________________
____Cassette Tape Player
____Piano
____Music Education Room
____Music Therapy Room

List music therapy needs of class:

Indicate time(s) available for music therapy:

MUSIC THERAPY REFERRAL CHECKLIST

CONFIDENTIAL INFORMATION

STUDENT____

Checklist completed by:______________________________Date:______________

____Has poor self-esteem or self-confidence
____Has difficulty following directions
____Has difficulty completing tasks independently
____Has difficulty staying in chair
____Pokes or hits other students frequently
____Talks out or disrupts frequently
____Has difficulty attending to the task at hand

____Maintains poor eye contact
____Does not participate readily in group activities
____Seldom initiates conversation
____Gives one-word or very short verbal responses to questions

____Has poor attitude as indicated by frequent negative verbalizations
____Has difficulty retaining information
____Has difficulty with tasks requiring auditory discrimination
____Has difficulty with gross motor tasks
____Has difficulty with fine motor tasks
____Has difficulty with receptive language
____Has difficulty with expressive language
____Lacks age-appropriate self-responsibilities
____Has difficulty with appropriate peer interaction
____Lacks age-appropriate concepts: ___colors ___shapes ___numbers ___time
___math ___rhyming ___sequencing
___directionality ___other:___________
____

Describe problems in the classroom related to the problems checked:_______
____
____
____

****

Background information

School:_____________________________ Teacher:______________________________

Grade:____________ Student's birthdate:_________________

Other related services:____

Qualification for special education services:_____________________________

Medical: Testing:

Family History:

Other:

SAMPLE

MUSIC THERAPY EVALUATION

CLIENT ______________________________ DATE ________________

DATE OF BIRTH ________________________ CAMPUS ______________

____ Client recommended for music therapy services

____ Client not recommended for music therapy services

____
Name
Music Therapist

SAMPLE

MUSIC THERAPY: ASSESSMENT SUMMARY

Name of Client: ______________________________

Agency: ______________________________

Date of Birth: ______________ Date of Evaluation: ______________

Parent(s)/Guardian(s): ______________________________

Home Address: ______________________________

Contact Person: ______________________________

Position of Contact Person: ______________________________

Reason for Referral:

Diagnosis:

Previous Test Information:

Music Therapy Evaluation Procedures:

Client's Reaction to Test Situation:

Evaluation Results:

Conclusions:

Recommendations:

______________ ______________

Date of Summary Music Therapist

SAMPLE

MUSIC THERAPY EVALUATION

NAME:____________________ DOB:____________ AGE:________

TEST DATE:__________________ EXAMINER:__________________

LOCATION:____

A. Clinical observation . . . . ☐
B. Evaluation . . . . ☐
C. Other:____________________ ☐

PROBLEM SUMMARY: This student demonstrated possible problems in the following area(s):

____ATTENTION
- ____Visual
- ____Auditory
- ____Task completion
- ____Perservation

____OCULAR MOTOR CONTROL
- ____Localization
- ____Tracking
- ____Midline usage
- ____Right, left differences

____VISUAL-MOTOR FUNCTIONING
- ____Eye-hand coordination
- ____Fine motor reproductions
- ____Organization of space

____AUDITORY FUNCTIONING
- ____Localization
- ____Discrimination
- ____Memory

____COMMUNICATION
- ____Receptive
- ____Expressive

____SOCIALIZATION
- ____Play
- ____Emotional expressions
- ____Personal responsibility

____GROSS MOTOR
- ____Coordination
- ____Motor planning
- ____Balance

OTHER COMMENTS:

RECOMMENDATIONS:
1. Music therapy services not recommended . . . ☐
2. Music therapy services recommended . . . . . ☐
   a. Direct services. . . . . ☐
   b. Consultative services. . . . . ☐
   c. Home programming . . . . ☐
   d. Other:____________________ ☐

ADDITIONAL INFORMATION NEEDED:

CLIENT INFORMATION

NAME_____________________________________ DATE______________________________

DATE OF BIRTH____________________________

I. GENERAL DESCRIPTION

II. FAMILY INFORMATION

III. MEDICAL HISTORY

IV. EDUCATIONAL HISTORY

V. TESTING

VI. RELATED SERVICES

____ Music Therapy
____ Psychological Services

____ Occupational Therapy
____ Speech Therapy

____ Physical Therapy
____ Other

SAMPLE

CASE HISTORY SUMMARY

NAME: HANDICAPPING CONDITION:

DATE OF BIRTH: AGE: DATE OF EVALUATION:

DIAGNOSIS:

MEDICAL:

ACADEMIC:

SOCIAL/BEHAVIORAL:

SENSORY SYSTEMS:

REFLEXES, REACTIONS:

TONE, STRENGTH, RANGE OF MOTION:

GROSS MOTOR:

FINE MOTOR:

SELF-HELP:

STRENGTHS: WEAKNESSES:

RECOMMENDATIONS:

____ MUSIC THERAPY ____ OCCUPATIONAL THERAPY ____ PHYSICAL THERAPY

COMMENTS:

CONFIDENTIAL INFORMATION
Page 1

SAMPLE

Music Therapy Assessment
Related Service Eligibility Report

NAME OF STUDENT: ______________________ DOB: __________

SCHOOL: ______________________ CLASS: __________

ASSESSMENT COMPLETED BY: Cathy Knoll, RMT-BC DATE: __________

* *

NATURE AND SEVERITY OF STUDENT'S PROBLEM. This student has difficulty in these areas:

	Therapist's Observation	Teacher's Observation	Stated on IEP
Reading			
Writing			
Mathematics			
Auditory perception			
Visual perception			
Awareness of self			
Classification			
Sequencing			
Time concepts			
Quantitative concepts			
Receptive language			
Expressive language			
Gross motor			
Fine motor			
Personal hygiene			
Dressing skills			
Eating skills			
Self-responsibility			
Interaction with others			
Impulse control			
Working independently			
Following directions			
Self-esteem			
Other:			
Other:			

COMMENTS:

☐ YES ☐ NO Based on my assessment, ______________________ does need music therapy in order to benefit from classroom instruction.

It is recommended that ______________________ receive (Indiv/group) music therapy services __________ a week for ______________________.

____
Catherine Dolan Knoll
Registered Music Therapist-Board Certified

SAMPLE

MUSIC THERAPY GOALS AND OBJECTIVES FOR IEP

The music therapy plan for this student will reinforce classroom goals and objectives. The anticipated instructional benefits include improved classroom functioning in the areas of cognition, language, motor skills, self-help skills, social/emotional functioning, creative expression, English and language arts, fine arts, and/or mathematics.

		PRE-TEST	PROGRESS
COGNITION AND MATHEMATICS	___Develops visual and aural memory ___Understands positional concepts ___Understands quantitative concepts ___Matches objects and symbols ___Classifies and sorts objects ___Repeats visual or auditory sequence ___Recognizes numerals ___Understands the concept of counting ___Other:		
RECEPTIVE LANGUAGE	___Learns meaning of objectives, action, descriptive, and position words ___Understands commands and questions ___Attends to stories and poems ___Other:		
EXPRESSIVE LANGUAGE	___Shows recognition of specific sounds ___Reproduces speech sounds ___Forms sounds into words ___Names objects ___Describes objects ___Asks and answers questions ___Forms simple sentences ___Uses complex sentences ___Other:		
ENGLISH/ LANGUAGE ARTS	___Attends and responds to oral communication ___Uses oral language to communicate effectively ___Develops vocabulary ___Develops comprehension skills ___Discriminates sounds ___Discriminates visual shapes, forms, letters ___Other:		

SAMPLE

		PRE-TEST	PROGRESS
GROSS AND FINE MOTOR; PHYSICAL EDUCATION	___Uses large muscle groups ___Tracks visually ___Grasps and releases objects ___Manipulates objects appropriately ___Develops eye-hand coordination ___Other:		
SELF-HELP	___Develops personal preference to be clean ___Demonstrates self-management in group ___Demonstrates self-responsibility ___Other:		
SOCIAL-EMOTIONAL	___Interacts with others ___Demonstrates positive social behaviors ___Listens to and follows directions ___Works independently ___Makes simple decisions and choices ___Demonstrates self-awareness and positive self-image ___Other:		
CREATIVE EXPRESSION; FINE ARTS	___Participates in organized dramatic play ___Develops body awareness and spatial perception using rhythmic and imitative movement ___Responds to music by listening ___Is able to create own music ___Produces music with voice ___Performs action songs and singing games ___Explores sound through instruments ___Plays instrument in ensemble ___Other:		
OTHER			

COMMENTS:

SAMPLE

INITIAL CONTACT WORKSHEET

TEACHER:

AIDE:

SCHOOL:

PRINCIPAL:

DIAGNOSTICIAN:

STUDENTS REFERRED BY TEACHER:

HIGH PRIORITY:

LOW PRIORITY:

SCHEDULE:

PREFERRED TIME:

LUNCH:

LIBRARY:

P.E.:

SPEECH:

OTHER SCHEDULED EVENTS:

SAMPLE

PROBLEM AND PROGRESS CHART

Client's Name ______________________ Date ______________

SKILLS (Ability Levels)	TYPICAL REACTIONS		BEST METHOD OF COPING BY STAFF (Procedure, Time Out, Rewards)
	Cooperative	Resistive	
A. DRESSING			
B. UNDRESSING			
C. TOILETING			
D. GROSS MOTOR PLAY			
E. FEEDING			
F. COMPREHENSION			
G. SPEECH			
H. SLEEPING HABITS			
I. OTHER			

Additional Comments:

SAMPLE

THE INDIVIDUALIZED EDUCATIONAL PLAN (IEP)

Student Name________________ Date of Birth__________ Age_______ Date of Program Entry__________

Local Education Agency________________ School____________________ Grade__________

SHORT TERM OBJECTIVES	STRATEGIES AND/OR TECHNIQUES	PERSONNEL RESPONSIBLE; MATERIALS AND/OR RESOURCES NEEDED	DATE STARTED	DATE ENDED	MASTERY CRITERIA	NOT WORKED ON	NO PROGRESS	EMERGING	SIGNIFICANT PROGRESS	ACHIEVEMENT	DATE EVALUATED

SAMPLE

INDIVIDUALIZED PROGRAM PLAN

Student Name (Last, First) ______

Team Leader ______

Date ______ DOB ______

Parent Contact ______

SERVICE AREA

OT ______
PT ______
MT ______
APE ______
SLH ______
HEALTH SERV. ______
ART ______

VOCATIONAL ______
WORK SHOP ______
FUNCTIONAL:
LANGUAGE ARTS ______
LIFE SKILLS ______
MATH ______

Goals:

Evaluation Code: X Introduced/not mastered, √ Mastered

Objectives: The student will:

Methods/Strategies

___monitor at least every 3 weeks
___one to one → small group
___independent learning opportunities
___redirection
___remediation
___repetition
___start below functional level
___increase difficulty in small steps
___help child compensate
___reinforce real effort
___positive feedback
___negotiation & offer choices

Behavior Management

___positive feedback
___reinforce real effort
___negotiation & offer choices
___selective ignoring
___remind of appropriate behavior
___confrontation
___redirection to stay on task
___time out
___contracts
___life space interview
___encourage verbalizing: feelings/needs

Materials

___programmed______
___basal______
___concrete______
___supplementary______
___remotivational______

Progress Notes:

SAMPLE

INDIVIDUAL SERVICE PLAN

Client (Last Name) (First Name) (Middle Initial)	Case Number

Date	
	A. Long Range Goal: B. Intermediate Objectives: C. Terms and Conditions: D. Client Participation, Cost of Services, and Use of Similar Benefits: E. Views of the Client: F. Criteria, Procedure, and Schedule for Review and Evaluation of Progress Toward Objectives and Goals: ______________________________ Name, Music Therapist

SAMPLE

GOAL PLANNING SHEET

STUDENT: ______________________ DATE: __________

GOAL: ______________________________________

____

ACTIVITY: ______________________________________

____

____

____

____

OBJECTIVE CRITERIA: ______________________________________

____

____

____

____

TEACHING STRATEGIES:

Behavior occurs:

____ Without prompt ____ With assistive device

____ With verbal prompt ____ With physical reinforcer

____ With physical prompt ____ Other:

Behavior does not occur:

____ Task too difficult: ______________________

____ Task needs task analysis: ______________________

____ Prompt or reinforcer inappropriate: ______________

COMMENTS:

Dellinda Henry
Registered Music Therapist

SAMPLE

MUSIC THERAPY TREATMENT PLAN - EARLY CHILDHOOD

Date:______________________________

School:______________________________

Code: 1) Group Activity = G
2) Individual Activity = I

PRE-ACADEMIC/ACADEMIC SKILLS

IMITATION SKILLS

GROSS MOTOR SKILLS

RECEPTIVE LANGUAGE SKILLS

AUDITORY PERCEPTUAL SKILLS

EXPRESSIVE LANGUAGE SKILLS

SOCIAL SKILLS

SAMPLE

- The Music Therapy Program Plan on page 115 was developed by Region 18 Education Service Center, Midland, TX for use in providing consultative services to special education classroom teachers.

- Since the consultant works with the direct care personnel as a teacher trainer, the consultant cannot be responsible for client progress. Therefore, goals, objectives, and criteria are written for the direct care personnel. Goals, objectives, and criteria for clients may also be prepared in order to assist the direct care provider.

- Signatures of both the direct care provider and the music therapy consultant imply cooperation in planning the program and add a sense of responsibility and obligation for the direct care provider to continue the program.

- This form is easily adapted for direct services by writing goals, objectives, and criteria that are client oriented rather than direct care provider oriented.

SAMPLE

MUSIC THERAPY PROGRAM PLAN

Name of Local Education Agency
Name of School Campus
Name of Classroom
Name of Teacher

Date

Goal: The teacher and aide will use a multi-sensory approach to address the areas of imitation, movement, and language.

Objectives: Students will (1) imitate others, (2) participate in group movement activities, (3) increase speech vocalization, (4) increase singing, and (5) follow directions.

Method: The teacher and aide will conduct a music group activity two times each week for fifteen minutes. A list of any activities used, but not provided by the Registered Music Therapist (RMT), will be maintained. The RMT will maintain a list of all activities disseminated to the teacher and aide. New activities will be demonstrated by the RMT. Preview records will be furnished to the teacher and aide as requested.

Evaluation Criteria for (Beginning Date) to (Ending Date):

____ Student A, ____ Student B, and ____ Student C will imitate actions to three familiar songs.

____ All students will participate in a minimum of three group movement activities during each music session.

____ Student A, ____ Student B, and ____ Student C will attempt to say important words in two music activities, such as up/down, in/out.

____ All other students will attempt to sing two familiar songs during each music session.

____ All students will perform simple motor movements according to verbal instructions provided by the teacher and/or aide.

/s/ by teacher

Name of Classroom Teacher

/s/ by RMT

Name of Registered Music Therapist
Region 18 Education Service Center
Midland, Texas

SAMPLE

MUSIC THERAPY PLANNING AND PROGRESS RECORD

Group:______________________________

Date:_______________________________

Therapist:__________________________

NAMES:							
GOAL: ACTIVITY:							
GOAL: ACTIVITY:							
GOAL: ACTIVITY:							
GOAL: ACTIVITY:							
GOAL: ACTIVITY:							
GOAL: ACTIVITY:							
GOAL: ACTIVITY:							
GOAL: ACTIVITY:							
GOAL: ACTIVITY:							
GOAL: ACTIVITY:							

M U S I C   T H E R A P Y

PROGRESS NOTES
Name, Registered Music Therapist

Date started: ______________

NAME: ______________________________ Date ended: ______________

Date	Notes

ATTENDANCE AND ACTIVITY CHART

Name: ______________________ Area: *Music Therapy*

Task															

Response key:

SAMPLE

MUSIC THERAPY PROGRESS SHEET DATE STARTED:__________ DATE ENDED:__________

Cathy Knoll, RMT-BC

STUDENT:____ CLASS:________________________

TARGET OBJECTIVE:

PROCEDURES/ACTIVITIES:

Baseline	Progress	Post Test

COMMENTS:

TARGET OBJECTIVE:

PROCEDURES/ACTIVITIES:

Baseline	Progress	Post Test

COMMENTS:

TARGET OBJECTIVE:

PROCEDURES/ACTIVITIES:

Baseline	Progress	Post Test

COMMENTS:

SAMPLE FORMAT

ACTIVITY HANDOUT

GOALS/PURPOSES FOR ACTIVITY:

OBJECTIVES OF ACTIVITY:

METHOD: (Copy of music activity)

VARIATIONS AND SUGGESTIONS FOR THE ACTIVITY:

SOURCE OF ACTIVITY:

SAMPLE

MUSIC ACTIVITIES
Early Childhood
1986-87

There are two purposes for an activity list such as the one shown below. The list assists the music therapist in planning sessions quickly once the list is prepared and it provides an easy check system on therapist job performance. As activities are demonstrated for direct care personnel or performed with clients the music therapist writes the date after the title. Another option is to divide activities into sections according to program plan goals and objectives.

CHANTS

Bear Hunt

Cabin in the Woods

Five Little Monkies

I Like

Oliver Twist

Stop, Look & Listen
9/14
Who Stole the Cookie from the Cookie Jar?

SINGING

Count with Me

Days of the Week

Did You Feed My Cow?

Five Angels

Five Little Pumpkins

Free Singing Activities

The Goat

Halloween is Coming

How Old Are You?
9/14
I Had a Little Overcoat

Kazoo activities

SINGING (cont.)

Mister Pibb

One of These Things

Pairs

Rock-A-My-Soul

Singing Top

Sweetly Sings the Donkey

What is Your Name?
9/14
Where is Mama ?
9/14
The Wind

You'll Sing a Song

FINE & GROSS MOTOR ACTIVITIES

Animal Antics

Bus Song
9/14
Clap Your Hands
9/14
Clapping Land

Enchiladas

MUSIC THERAPY PROGRESS RECORD

Cathy Knoll, RMT-BC

CLIENT:__________________________ PERIOD COVERED: From____________ to ____________

This client's music therapy plan will include learning experiences and procedures to reinforce skills in the following areas of need as specified in his/her Individualized Program Plan (IPP).

AREA OF NEED	GOAL	PRE-TEST	PROGRESS
MOBILITY	1. Discriminating left from right	1.	1.
PRE-VOCATIONAL	1. Arriving on time	1.	1.
	2. Attending to task with distraction	2.	2.
	3. Following work routine	3.	3.
	4. Interacting appropriately with others	4.	4.
	5. Completing task within time limit	5.	5.
	6. Following multi-step instruction	6.	6.
PERSONAL AND SOCIAL ADJUSTMENT	1. Demonstrating self-control in group	1.	1.
	2. Discriminating fact and opinion	2.	2.
	3. Listening attentively	3.	3.
	4. Discriminating opinion and fact	4.	4.
READING AND WRITING	1. Identifying traffic signs and symbols	1.	1.
	2. Copying letters of the alphabet	2.	2.
	3. Printing name	3.	3.
	4. Printing address	4.	4.
	5. Writing name cursively	5.	5.
	6. Copying printed material	6.	6.
COMMUNICATION	1. Relating personal data	1.	1.
	2. Eye contact when listening	2.	2.
	3. Eye contact when speaking	3.	3.
	4. Using social speech	4.	4.
	5. Describing events in sequence	5.	5.
	6. Asking questions	6.	6.
	7. Answering open-ended questions	7.	7.
	8. Participating in group discussions	8.	8.
	9. Speaking in complete sentences	9.	9.

SAMPLE

MUSIC THERAPY, Page 2

AREA OF NEED	GOAL	PRE-TEST	PROGRESS
TIME	1. Naming days of the week	1.	1.
	2. Naming months of year	2.	2.
	3. Identifying present, past, next year	3.	3.
	4. Reading day, month, year on calendar	4.	4.
	5. Reading hour on clock	5.	5.
	6. Reading half hour on clock	6.	6.
ARITHMETIC	1. Counting objects	1.	1.
	2. Writing numerals	2.	2.
	3. Recognizing and naming numerals	3.	3.
	4. Matching quantity to number symbols	4.	4.
	5. Sequencing numbers	5.	5.
HYGIENE	1. Wearing appropriate clothing	1.	1.
OTHER MUSIC THERAPY GOALS	1. Demonstrating self-responsibility	1.	1.
	2. Developing positive self-image	2.	2.
	3. Improving visual memory	3.	3.
	4. Improving auditory memory	4.	4.
	5. Understanding positional concepts	5.	5.
	6. Repeating visual or aural sequence	6.	6.
	7. Discriminating sounds	7.	7.
	8. Developing eye-hand coordination	8.	8.
	9. Participating in organized programs	9.	9.
	10. Playing instruments in ensemble	10.	10.
	11. Singing in ensemble	11.	11.

COMMENTS:

SAMPLE

- The therapist could keep numerous copies of this form available to use in different situations.

- To record individual and group progress:

Objective #1 To decrease talking out-of-turn	Sally	John	Terri	Suzie	Kent	class total
Pre-test (9/15)	𝍸 𝍸	𝍸 ||||	𝍸 𝍸 |	||||	𝍸 ||||	42
Post-test (5/7	||||	|||	|||	||	|	13

- To record individual progress:

	♩	𝅗𝅥	♫	𝄽	𝄞 C	𝅝
Date Introduced	9/14	9/23	9/25		9/14	
Date mastered	10/05	10/05	10/12		9/17	

- To reinforce individuals for appropriate behavior:

	GOOD LISTENERS 9/15/					
Justin	☺	☺	☹	☺	☺	
Robert	☹	☹	☹	☺	☺	

MULTI-PURPOSE FORM

SAMPLE

MUSIC THERAPY DATA SHEET
Kathleen A. Coleman, RMT-BC

Client: ____________________
Location: ____________________

Reinforcers: ____________________
____

OBJECTIVE	TASKS	DATE		DATE		DATE		DATE		DATE		DATE		DATE		DATE	
		TP	CR	TP	CR	TP	CR	TP	CR	TP	CR	TP	CR	TP	CR	TP	CR

Code: Therapist Prompt (TP):
G = Gross physical
P = Partial physical
M = Model
RV = Repeated verbal
V = Verbal

Client Response (CR):
A = Active refusal
O = Incorrect response
- = Incomplete response
+ = Complete/correct response
/ = Task not included that day

INTERIM REPORT

Client:

Report Prepared by:

Date:

I. Results of Initial Evaluation

II. Goal and Objectives Established as Result of Evaluation:

III. Strategies/Criteria for Success:

Comments:

SAMPLE

INTERIM REPORT

Client:

Report Prepared by:

Date:

Target Objective 1:

Procedures:

Target Objective 2:

Procedures:

Target Objective 3:

Procedures:

Target Objective 4:

Procedures:

Comments:

MUSIC THERAPY PROGRESS REPORT

CLIENT ______________________________ DATE OF INITIATION ___________

____

____

____

____

____

____

____

____

____

____

____

____

____

____

____

____

____

____

____

____

____

____

Name, Music Therapist

SAMPLE

MUSIC THERAPY SEMESTER REPORT

____
date

Client:

Placement:

Date of first session:

Target behavior(s): Progress:

Comments:

Recommendations:

____
Music Therapist

SAMPLE

Report of Individual Progress
In A Group Therapy Situation

I. The following are target areas defined for all of the group members:

A. Target Objective:
Procedure:
Progress:

B. Target Objective:
Procedure:
Progress:

C. Target Objective:
Procedure:
Progress:

D. Target Objective:
Procedure:
Progress:

II. The following are target areas defined for individual members of the therapy group:

A. Client's Name:

Target Objective:
Procedure:
Progress:

Target Objective:
Procedure:
Progress:

B. Client's Name:

Target Objective:
Procedure:
Progress:

Target Objective:
Procedure:
Progress:

SAMPLE

Cathy Knott REGISTERED MUSIC THERAPIST

Box T428 Stephenville, Texas 76402 817/968-2882

Dear (teacher's name) :

I will not be attending individual Admission, Review, Dismissal (ARD) meetings of your students because of the time it would take away from direct service with the students. However, I will be more than happy to make arrangements to attend any ARD meeting at which you feel I might make a specific contribution. The following comments summarize group progress for this year.

The primary target objective for these students has been developing "classroom survival" skills. As a result of a behavioral program, marked improvement has been noted in this area. In September, strong contingencies were required to help the students control their behavior. By April, occasional social reinforcement and reminders of the "rules" were enough to maintain control.

Date	Verbal Interruptions*	Following Directions*	Completing Assignments Independently*	Negative Peer Interactions*
September (baseline)	47	50%	10%	35
April	4	80%	75%	7

*class average during a 30 minute session

R___ has a great deal of difficulty comprehending directions and retaining information as well as with auditory and motor tasks. T____ has shown a marked decrease in negative comments about himself and now converses more appropriately. S____ requires more specific contingencies than the other students to maintain appropriate group behavior. D____ talks a great deal, but not in a disruptive manner. He appears to have a low frustration tolerance. M____, T_____, and C____ have developed better than average guitar skills. J__ responds well to contingencies. His behavior has improved with his new classroom placement. L_____ has shown improvement in the fine motor skills required to play the guitar, but more work is needed in this area.

"a program responsive to special needs"

FINAL REPORT

PREPARED BY:
PERIOD COVERED:

CLIENT:
DATE OF BIRTH:

BACKGROUND INFORMATION:

INITIAL OBSERVATIONS: DATE:

Target Objective 1:

Procedure:

Progress:

Target Objective 2:

Procedure:

Progress:

Target Objective 3:

Procedure:

Progress:

COMMENTS AND RECOMMENDATIONS:

SAMPLE

MUSIC THERAPY DISCHARGE SUMMARY

Client____________________ Date____________________

Date of Birth________________ Campus____________________

Name
Registered Music Therapist

TERMINATION REPORT

CLIENT:

AGENCY:

DATE OF REPORT:

PERIOD COVERED:

REPORT SUBMITTED BY:

ATTITUDES TOWARD SELF/OTHERS:

PRIORITIES AND GOALS REACHED:

GOALS REQUIRING ADDITIONAL WORK:

RECOMMENDATIONS:

April, 1982

Dear Parents:

Thank you for your assistance in completing this music therapy questionnaire. Its purpose is simply to help me know what types of music your child may be familiar with so I may plan activities which best meet their educational needs. If you have any questions, feel free to contact me.

Sincerely,

Kathleen A. Coleman, RMT
Music Therapist

MUSIC THERAPY QUESTIONNAIRE

1. Do you have a record player or tape player in your home? yes/no

2. Does your child listen to records or tapes? yes/no

3. If so, does he/she have any particular favorites? yes/no

List:____

____

____

4. Do you have a television in your home? yes/no

5. If so, does your child have a favorite program? yes/no

List:____

____

____

6. Do you have a radio in your home? yes/no

7. If so, does your child have a particular radio station he/she listens to? yes/no

List:____

8. Are there any other radio stations your family listens to frequently? yes/no

   List:______________________________

9. Do you have any musical instruments in your home? yes/no

10. If so, what instruments do you have and who plays them?

    List:______________________________

    ____

11. Does anyone in your family sing in a choir or participate in some type of organized musical group? (i.e., community symphony or church choir, etc.) yes/no

12. If so, what types of groups do they participate in?

    List:______________________________

    ____

13. Does your child sing along with the songs on the radio or T.V.? yes/no

14. Have you observed your child singing a song when neither the television or radio is on? yes/no

15. Does your child have some favorite songs? yes/no

16. If so, what are the titles of these songs?

    List:______________________________

    ____

17. Do any of your children take lessons on a musical instrument? yes/no

18. Do you and your family attend musical activities in the church or community? yes/no

19. Does your child have any musical toys? yes/no

    List:______________________________

    ____

20. Is there anything about your child's recreational or musical behavior that you think would help me better understand your child?

    ____

    ____

Address
Date

Dear Parent:

Your child can accomplish much through our mutual cooperation and assistance. The students who achieve the most are those who follow a systematic study plan and who have incentives and goals to work for. Therefore, throughout the year I will be evaluating your child's progress and make any revisions that will assist the child in achieving their potential.

There are a few suggestions I would like to share with you:

1. Have a regular practice time (preferably divided into shorter periods for the beginning student). The time should be agreed upon by pupil and parents and then adhered to. If possible the piano and T.V. should not be in the same room.
2. Reward your child's study by sitting down and listening to the assignment occasionally. Give more encouragement than criticism.
3. See that your child brings the music to each lesson. A heavy folder or case will protect the music from wear, loss, and weather.

Tuition will be charged at a monthly rate. The nine month's tuition has been prorated for easy budgeting. School holidays such as Labor Day, Thanksgiving, Christmas, and Easter have not been charged for. During the nine months there will be no makeup lessons as some months have an extra lesson for which you are not charged. In event of illness over a period of more than two weeks, makeup lessons will be scheduled.

Your bill will be presented in ample time so that it may be paid in advance, not later than the 10th of each month. All students are expected to enroll for the full nine months of the year. If a student must quit due to illness, moving, or parent/teacher/student agreement, one month's notice is required and/or one month's tuition.

In closing, I feel that every parent is entitled to know my professional background and training. My service brochure is enclosed for your review.

If you have any questions, concerns, or suggestions during the year please call me. I always make myself available for conferences. Occasional visits to observe your child's lesson are also recommended.

Sincerely,

Name, RMT-BC

MEMO

TO: Parents of music therapy students

FROM:

DATE:

SUBJECT: Music therapy services

General Information: During the first session I will assess your child in the following areas: communication, gross and fine motor, attention span, concentration, thinking and learning styles, imitation, emotional expression, and self-control. As soon as possible each parent will receive a music therapy program plan outlining the goals and objectives for the child. After the parent reviews the program plan, I will answer any questions and explain or demonstrate activities I use to assist the student in achieving the goals and objectives. I encourage parents to share the information with their child's teachers.

Class Schedule: Sessions will be held on Tuesday evenings from 7:00 to 8:00 p.m. The first session begins on Tuesday, September 4.

Location: The sessions will be held at my home so that we can use the piano and other equipment. The address is 1314 West 81st Street. A map is attached for your benefit.

Fees: A monthly charge of $________ is payable at the first session of each month. Parents must provide their own transportation.

IF YOU HAVE ANY QUESTIONS OR CONCERNS, PLEASE CALL ME AT 359-0033. HOPE TO SEE YOU ON SEPTEMBER 4 AT 7:00 p.m.

SAMPLE

Date

Name of Parent
Address
City, State Zip

Re: Music Therapy Program for (name of student)

Dear Parents:

During each music therapy session, __________ has shown improvement. Based on the information gained during the previous music therapy sessions, the following goals and objectives are targeted for _________.

Cognitive Skills:
1.
2.
3.

Communication Skills:
1.
2.
3.

Gross Motor and Fine Motor Skills:
1.
2.
3.

Listening Skills:
1.
2.
3.

Music Skills:
1.
2.
3.

Reading Foundations:
1.
2.
3.

If you have any questions or concerns, please contact me prior to the next session. I will continue to evaluate _________ so that I may serve him better. _________ is a pleasure to work with!

Name
Registered Music Therapist-
Board Certified

SAMPLE

Note: Graph paper is economical and saves time in keeping attendance.

NAME	DATE 9/5	9/12	9/19	9/26	10/3	10/10
Sara	✓	✓	a	✓	a	✓
Maynon	✓	a	✓	✓	✓	a
Travis	✓	✓	✓	✓	✓	✓
Martha	✓	✓	✓	✓	✓	✓
Count	✓	✓	✓	a	✓	✓

MATERIALS CHECK-OUT LIST

Materials	Loaned	Received	Materials	Loaned	Received

SAMPLE

CONSULTANT LOG

DATE: CONSULTANT:

FACILITY: ADDRESS:

Date	Arrival Time	Departure Time	Direct Care Provider	Task for the Day

CONSULTANT LOG

DATE: CONSULTANT:

FACILITY: ADDRESS:

Date	Arrival Time	Departure Time	Direct Care Provider	Evalu-ation	Confer-ence	Demon-stration	Other

QUARTERLY SERVICE SUMMARY

MUSIC THERAPY

Reporting Period: ________________ to ________________
(date) (date)

Summary	Current Period	Year to Date
Referrals	________	________
Clients receiving services	________	________
Clients showing documented progress	________	________
Total number music therapy sessions	________	________
Total number music therapy hours	________	________

Comments:

____

Name, Music Therapist

SAMPLE

CONSULTATIVE SERVICES SUMMARY

LEA/SCHOOL________________ CLASS________________ TEACHER________________

Initial School Visit________________ Referral Form Completed________________

Initial Classroom Observations																								
Demonstrations																								
Material Previews																								
Music Therapy Plan/Revisions																								
Teacher Observations by RMT																								
MT Plan/Progress Evaluations																								
Consultation: LEA Staff																								
Consultation: ESC Staff																								

Comments:

Note: A summary such as this aids the consultant in monitoring program status. The music therapist indicates by date which consultative services were used on each visit. This form was developed by Region 18 Education Service Center, Midland, Texas.

SAMPLE FLOWCHART

PROVISION OF CONTRACTUAL CONSULTATIVE SERVICES

STEPS	DESCRIPTION	FORMS
REFERRAL ↓	Special education or music education teachers interested in receiving consultative music therapy services are provided by agency administration.	None
STAFF ORIENTATION ↓ (→ Services not accepted.)	An overview of music therapy and potential services is presented to the participating personnel. Information outlining usual responsibilities of the agency staff is disseminated.	Presentation Handouts
CONTRACTING ↓	The education agency and music therapist complete a contract outlining service(s), reimbursement(s), and responsibilities of all participating personnel.	Contract Statements
SCREENING ↓ (→ Referral deemed inappropriate.)	The music therapist observes each referred teacher and their students to determine programming needs and initial activities. The referral is reviewed with the referring source.	Music Therapy Referral and Assessment Summary
SERVICES ↓ (→ Services are no longer requested or appropriate.)	School personnel and the music therapist set a starting date for services and schedule school visits. Throughout the school year, the music therapist will provide the following services to teachers and their students: 1. Informal assessment 2. Program planning 3. Demonstrations and explanation materials of activities and techniques 4. Assistance with selection and adaptation of materials and equipment 5. Observation of teachers during music activities 6. Workshops, as requested The music therapist maintains a class folder located in the school district's files. The music therapist will provide quarterly reports and consultative service hour verification to administrators.	Classroom Folder Folder Checkout M.T.R.A. Summary Program Plans Activities List Activity Handouts Materials Checkout Materials Preview Sheet Quarterly Reports

This form was developed by Region 18 Education Service Center, Midland, Texas.

SAMPLE

LETTER TO A NEW TEACHER

Date

Teacher's Name
Department or Campus
Name of School District
Address
City, State Zip

Dear Name:

Welcome to your new teaching position! Associated Consultants provides various services to your school district through contractual arrangements.

During the past school year, music therapy services were received by the teacher and students in your classroom. These music therapy services are now available to you. Information about the program is enclosed for your review. Please read the information carefully and then decide if you wish to continue these services. As you will see, all my efforts hinge on your follow-through of the activities.

Our first school visit is scheduled for __________. At that time I will answer any questions you may have about the services. If it is your desire to begin a music therapy program, I will observe and evaluate your students, individually and collectively. I will also review your goals, objectives, and activities so we can begin a music therapy program as soon as possible.

May your new year be a successful and rewarding one!

Sincerely,

Name
Music Therapy Consultant

Enclosures

SAMPLE

LETTER OF GOODWILL

Date

Name
Title
Agency
Address

Dear Name:

Once again you have shown true administrative support for music therapy. During our recent conference with the special education department, you were so helpful to me. Your input regarding administrative concerns was extremely beneficial to the other administrators.

After the conference was over, I realized how far music therapy has come in your program. Five years ago you were asking me for information and today you are giving information to other programs. I see now that I must plan a music therapy overview for the new teaching staff. As our goals for the music therapy program have changed through the years, I overlooked the importance of explaining what I do and why music therapy is offered. I will send information out to all the new principals immediately.

The concerns you had about the staff at Mason school have all been resolved. We have discussed all our options for the schedule. The teachers have selected times which are beneficial to all. I explained what my own responsibilities were and gave them copies of the flowchart. I think they will be able to contact the appropriate person about any future problems. They seem to feel much better and have been more open and communicative since they know who is responsible for what. Naturally, it was a BIG relief to learn they do have control over their own schedules and that problems would be resolved.

I hope we will continue our successful and mutually supportive working relationship in the years to come.

Sincerely,

RMT

SAMPLE

Date

Dear (Teacher's name):

The music therapy schedule for the _______ year in _____________ is as follows:

8:30 Intermediate Self-Contained Class
9:15 Resource Class
10:00 Elementary Self-Contained Class
10:45 Early Childhood Class
11:30 Resource Class

An information sheet about music therapy as a related service is attached. It is important to note that music activities are used as a tool by the therapist to set the occasion for helping each student reach non-musical goals. Music therapy should reinforce skills being developed in the classroom. Although the music is enjoyable, the program's primary purpose is to give each student assistance in skills development.

Please feel free to comment on areas of need. Because I only see the students once a week, your verbal input is essential for an effective music therapy program.

If you need written reports or progress notes during the year, please let me know. Thanks for your support.

____

Music Therapist

Enclosures: Objectives of the Music Therapy Program
Music Therapy Information Sheet

Page Two, Name of Teacher

Objectives of the Music Therapy Program

1. To develop programs for reaching individual goals as described on each student's Individual Education Plan (IEP).

2. To develop programs for reinforcing skills learned in the classroom. Some of the target areas we will be working on during the year include:
   a. Classroom survival skills (directions, attention span, task completion, etc.)
   b. Verbal skills
   c. Gross motor and visual motor skills
   d. Auditory perception
   e. Self-identification
   f. Self-confidence
   g. Listening and impulse control
   h. Interpersonal relationships

   Each student has specific target objectives, based upon their IEP, the therapist's assessment of his needs, and recommendations from the teacher and other related professionals.

3. To develop each child's musical interests and skills. A music therapist is trained to develop music programs for students with special needs.

4. To provide consultation with the classroom and/or resource teacher in these areas as requested:
   a. Classroom management
   b. Behavioral programs or skills development programs
   c. Music activities appropriate for functioning level of students

5. To work in cooperation with other related services personnel.

Music Therapy Services

Music therapists work with individuals or groups of students with physical, behavioral, developmental, and/or perceptual problems. Developmental, corrective, supportive, and/or evaluative services provided include the following:

1. Participating as a member of the treatment team or ARD team.
2. Conducting initial assessment of each student.
3. Establishing specific objectives for the IEP to support classroom goals.
4. Establishing specific procedures to reach treatment objectives.
5. Conducting therapy sessions with individuals or small groups.
6. Remediating specific handicapping conditions.
7. Generalizing newly-learned behavioral patterns to classroom situations.
8. Consulting with teachers and other related services personnel.
9. Programming music skills for students with specific disabilities.
10. Consulting with parents on student's progress and suggested home programs.
11. Evaluating and reporting each student's progress.

SAMPLE

STUDENT PROGRESS REPORT

____
Date

____
Student Name

	Sept.	Oct.	Nov.	Dec.
Listened to and followed directions				
Cooperated well with others				
Completed assignments independently				
Assumed responsibility for self and belongings				

Comments:

____
Music Therapist

This Student Progress Report was adapted from a sample report located in <u>Strategies for Effective Parent-Teacher Interaction, A Guide for Teacher Trainers</u>. (For information contact Roger Kroth, Department of Special Education, University of New Mexico, Albuquerque, New Mexico.)

PHOTO RELEASE

______ I give my permission for photos of ______________________________
to be used in educational publications and presentations.

______ I do not give my permission for photos of ______________________
to be used.

____

Signature of Guardian

____

Date

- -

RELEASE OF INFORMATION

______ I give permission for information in the file of ________________
____________________ to be released to __________________________

for use in developing a therapy plan.

______ I do not give permission for release of information.

____

Signature of Guardian

____

Date

Success in a career means different things to different people. Most people work primarily for financial gain. A career might also be pursued for opportunities to serve others, for personal growth, and for personal satisfaction. A person can be considered successful in his career if he utilizes his gifts and talents while balancing personal and professional priorities. Managing time efficiently, channeling stress, and communicating effectively with others through networking are critical to career success.

DEFINING GOALS AND PRIORITIES

Taking time to clarify specific goals and objectives gives purpose and direction to each day, leading to greater personal satisfaction and a sense of achievement. One must analyze past life experiences, current values and motivations, on-going dreams and fantasies, areas of strengths and weaknesses, current commitments and needs, and personal and professional philosophies and priorities before defining goals. The questions and charts in Chapter 1 will guide this self-analysis.

Although professional and personal goals are interrelated, separating the two areas is advised for clarity. A worksheet for each target area is helpful. A sample "Goals and Objectives" Worksheet is located on page 160. Once goals are established, concentrate on those priorities and make no apologies for neglected areas. Periodic review of short-term and long-term goals helps concentrate time and energy. Having established specific goals helps in the effectiveness of another key to success, time management.

TIME MANAGEMENT

Time is a resource. But unlike many other resources, we cannot buy it, borrow it, save it or otherwise change it. All we can do is spend it or invest it. Yet many of us focus our thoughts on trying to save time instead of focusing on better ways to spend it.

The first step in effective time management is evaluating the ways in which time is currently spent. Document activities for several days on a chart similar to that found on page 161, then adjust time allotments for personal and professional activities according to goal priorities. Each week list tasks by priority and schedule tasks in a weekly plan. Begin each day with a review of the day's schedule, making revisions where necessary. Samples of planning pages are located on pages 162 and 163.

When tempted to alter the daily plan, make certain top priorities and critical tasks are not set aside. Flexibility is necessary in daily living, but eliminating time wasters is helpful in decreasing frustration.

YOUR TIME BUDGET

Take time to **think**; it is the foundation of **WISDOM.**

Take time to **read**; it is a source of **POWER.**

Take time to **laugh**; it's the music of the **SOUL.**

Take time to **dream**; it's like hitching your wagon to a **STAR.**

Take time to **love**; it is the highest **JOY OF LIFE.**

BUT ALSO REMEMBER

Take time to **work**; it's the price of **SUCCESS.**

Anonymous

STRESS MANAGEMENT

Stress is pressure resulting from dealing with situations in daily work. With proper management, stress can be a positive motivator that encourages people to think and act creatively when facing problems. Stress overload can lead to frustration and burnout, making a person feel totally at odds with his job. Factors contributing to this feeling include:

- Absence of adequate support network or outside interests
- Boredom or lack of motivation
- Conflicting goals or values among staff or with administrators
- Continuous adjustments and/or adaptations
- Inadequate salary or other financial burdens
- Infrequent opportunities to exchange ideas with other music therapists
- Lack of negotiation on important issues
- Lack of organizational or time management skills
- Over-supervision or lack of administrative support or direction
- Problems or pressures in personal life
- Unreasonable work loads or schedules

The key to successful stress management is having options in coping with sources of stress. After clearly defining the specific problem, list all alternative solutions, evaluate each option, then move forward to resolve the situation. When working with administrators, for example, document information thoroughly so as to present needs in a rational business-like manner. When appropriate, request personal involvement in policy making and issues clarification.

Keep in mind that on occasion, stress can be a positive factor that serves to end procrastination, aid in creativity, and lead to lively conversations that open channels of communication. There are times, however, that stress-related problems cannot be overcome. If that is the case, carefully study all alternatives. If a job change is the only solution, then take that step and begin again.

NETWORKING

Networking is the process of communicating with friends, family, and other contacts for information, advice, and moral support while pursuing a career. Learning to locate, utilize, develop, and share resources is vital to professional success.

There are many ways to develop contacts with other professionals. Writing notes to co-workers, colleagues, guest speakers, conference organizers, and other active professionals is an effective way to say thank you, offer a word of encouragement, or express your opinion on a specific issue.

Attending professional conferences and seminars enables music therapists to keep in touch with current techniques, trends, and legislative concerns. Such meetings provide opportunities to meet colleagues in music therapy and related fields. Exchanging business cards and following up with a brief note to colleagues who are interested in communicating will expand your network.

Take time to observe music therapists and professionals in related fields at work. Share ideas, interesting materials, and successful techniques with others through workshops, informal sharing sessions, articles in regional journals, or meetings of area music therapists. Organize groups of music therapists if none are currently active in the local area.

As a citizen and music therapist in the community, it is necessary to keep abreast of local and national affairs. Include elected officials in your network. Keep informed of local community activities and attend citizens' and public interest meetings. Work with organizations that support or provide social services to your community. Let elected representatives know your thoughts on issues that impact music therapy or your clients. In conclusion, it is essential that you "know your community" and "communicate with your community" in order to create a successful network. The following lists will be helpful.

Know your community:

- Accrediting agencies
- Agency personnel
- Community organizations
- Competitors
- Consumers of services
- Federal agencies
- Health agencies
- Physicians, psychiatrists, psychologists
- Politicians
- Potential consumers
- Professional organizations
- State agencies

Communicate with your community:

- Annual and monthly reports
- Brochures
- Business cards
- Conferences
- Mail
- Mass media
- Newsletters
- Personal contacts
- Posters
- Professional journals
- Speakers bureau
- Special projects
- Telephone

FINAL NOTE

Success is attainable by all those who actively seek it. Each person must define goals, then work diligently to reach those goals. As Eleanor Roosevelt said, "Some people succeed by great talent, some by the influence of friends, some by a miracle. But the majority succeed by hard work."

SUGGESTIONS FOR FURTHER READING

Bliss, E.C. (1976). Getting things done: The ABC's of time management. New York, NY: Scribner.

Fanning, T. & Fanning, R. (1979). Get it all done and still be human. Radnor, PA: Chilton.

Lakein, A. (1974). How to get control of your time and your life. New York, NY: The New American Library, Inc.

Le Boeuf, M. (1980). Working smart. New York, NY: Warner Books, Inc.

Rohn, J. (Speaker). (1985). Success -- The seven strategies. (Cassette Tape Series). Chicago, IL: Nightingale-Conant Corporation.

Welch, M. (1981). Networking. New York, NY: Warner Books, Inc.

Winston, S. (1981). Getting organized: Storage. New York, NY: Warner Books, Inc.

Winston, S. (1978). Getting organized: The easy way to put your life in order. New York, NY: Norton.

SAMPLE

GOALS AND OBJECTIVES WORKSHEET

GOAL:______________________________ DATE:__________

1. Objective:________________________ Target Date:__________

   Criteria for Success:________________________

   Procedure:______________________________

   ____

   Update:______________________________

   ____

   Objective Reached ______

2. Objective:________________________ Target Date:__________

   Criteria for Success:________________________

   Procedure:______________________________

   ____

   Update:______________________________

   ____

   Objective Reached ______

3. Objective:________________________ Target Date:__________

   Criteria for Success:________________________

   Procedure:______________________________

   ____

   Update:______________________________

   ____

   Objective Reached ______

SAMPLE

EVALUATION OF TIME MANAGEMENT

Name________________________ Day______________ Date______________

Time	Activity	Importance	Interruptions	
			Phone	Other
7:00		1 2 3 4 5		
7:30		1 2 3 4 5		
8:00		1 2 3 4 5		
8:30		1 2 3 4 5		
9:00		1 2 3 4 5		
9:30		1 2 3 4 5		
10:00		1 2 3 4 5		
10:30		1 2 3 4 5		
11:00		1 2 3 4 5		
11:30		1 2 3 4 5		
12:00		1 2 3 4 5		
12:30		1 2 3 4 5		
1:00		1 2 3 4 5		
1:30		1 2 3 4 5		
2:00		1 2 3 4 5		
2:30		1 2 3 4 5		
3:00		1 2 3 4 5		
3:30		1 2 3 4 5		
4:00		1 2 3 4 5		
4:30		1 2 3 4 5		
5:00		1 2 3 4 5		
5:30		1 2 3 4 5		
6:00		1 2 3 4 5		
6:30		1 2 3 4 5		

SAMPLE

WEEKLY TIME MANAGEMENT SHEET
for the week of ________

Personal	Family	Church Sun.Sch.	Organizations	House	Music Works	Business	Planning & Preparation	Groceries	Special Projects
			Delta K.G.				Private		
			EARC				Foster Home		
			PTA				SISD		
			Little Thea.				GISD		
			C. Chorale				ICFMR		

MONDAY	TUESDAY	WEDNESDAY	THURSDAY	FRIDAY	SATURDAY	SUNDAY

Weekly Objectives:

Date____________________

TO DO:	PRIORITY	DONE

TIME	SUNDAY	MONDAY	TUESDAY	WEDNESDAY	THURSDAY	FRIDAY	SATURDAY
8:00							
8:30							
9:00							
9:30							
10:00							
10:30							
11:00							
11:30							
12:00							
12:30							
1:00							
1:30							
2:00							
2:30							
3:00							
3:30							
4:00							
4:30							
5:00							
5:30							
6:00							
6:30							
7:00							
7:30							
8:00							
8:30							
9:00							
9:30							
10:00							

ABOUT THE AUTHORS

DELLINDA HENRY, RMT-BC graduated with honors from West Texas State University in Canyon, TX. After completing her internship at Sunshine/Sertoma Learning Center in Knoxville, TN, Dellinda remained on staff as music therapist. In 1979, Dellinda returned to Texas and established a consultative music therapy program at Region 18 Education Service Center in Midland. She now resides in Austin, TX where she is self-employed and contracts with programs for the hearing impaired and deaf-blind multihandicapped.

Dellinda provides temporary parenting to children with a variety of needs in her licensed therapeutic foster home. Dellinda has one child, Jamie, a young man with deafness and blindness. Dellinda is an active member of the Deaf-Blind Multihandicapped Association of Texas, a parent/professional organization. She serves as Editor of the Association newsletter. Dellinda presents numerous workshops at family and professional conferences.

Dellinda studies traditional Tai Chi, karate, self-defense, and philosophy under the instruction of an 18th generation Inja.

CATHERINE DOLAN KNOLL, RMT-BC received her degree in music therapy with honors from Texas Woman's University and completed her internship at the Cleveland Music School Settlement. Previous work experience includes working on staff at the Cleveland Music School Settlement and developing a music therapy program at Texas Center for the Blind in Kerrville, TX. Cathy currently serves private clients and contracts music therapy services to public school programs, intermediate care facilities, and a foster care facility in the Stephenville, Texas area.

Cathy is an active member of the National Association for Music Therapy serving on the education committee and the ad hoc finance committee. She has presented numerous conference workshops and published articles in regional and national professional journals.

Cathy is active in the Stephenville Area Little Theatre, Delta Kappa Gamma, the Cross Timbers Civic Chorale, the Erath County Association for Retarded Citizens, and is a Vice-President of the Chamberlain PTA. Cathy and her husband, Ed, have two children, Tommy and Dwight.

BARBARA REUER, MME, RMT-BC received her undergraduate degree in music education from Northern State College (South Dakota), her master's degree and music therapy equivalency from the University of Kansas, and is currently completing her doctoral work at the University of Iowa. Her dissertation research is "An Evaluation of the Present National Association for Music Therapy (NAMT) Curriculum in View of Clinical, Academic, and Regulatory Criteria." Barbara has worked at the University of Iowa as Acting Director of Music Therapy and visiting instructor. Her clinical experience in music therapy includes work at mental health facilities, forensic units, and public school special education programs.

Barbara is an active member of NAMT both at the national and regional levels, currently serving on the Assembly of Delegates, a national task force, and as the Midwestern Regional President.

Barbara has owned and operated her multi-level marketing business for eight years, giving her invaluable marketing and management experience. Barbara is active in community organizations, enjoys reading, and is a competitive racquet ball player.